Cook's Corner

Brilliant
Barbecue

igloobooks

Published in 2018
by Igloo Books Ltd
Cottage Farm
Sywell
NN6 0BJ
www.igloobooks.com

Food photography and recipe development:
© Stockfood, The Food Media Agency
Cover image: © iStock / Getty Images
Additional imagery: © iStock / Getty Images

STA002 0218
2 4 6 8 10 9 7 5 3 1
ISBN: 978-1-78810-173-8

Cover designed by Nicholas Gage
Interiors designed by Simon Parker
Edited by Jasmin Peppiatt

Printed and manufactured in China

Cook's Corner

Brilliant
Barbecue

Contents

Cook's Corner

Brilliant Barbecue

Meat dishes

Lamb burger

SERVES: 4 | PREP TIME: 25-30 MINUTES | COOKING TIME: 25 MINUTES

INGREDIENTS

800 g / 1 lb 12 oz / 4 cups lean lamb mince

50 g / 2 oz Parmesan, finely grated

1 tsp Worcestershire sauce

4 sesame seed buns, halved

tomato ketchup

4 large lettuce leaves

METHOD

1. Preheat the barbecue to a moderately hot temperature.

2. Mix together the lean lamb mince, Parmesan, Worcestershire sauce, salt and ground black pepper in a large mixing bowl.

3. Divide the mixture into eight balls and shape each one into burgers.

4. Cook the burgers on the barbecue for 12-14 minutes, turning once after around 7 minutes, until fully cooked.

5. Meanwhile, spread the bottom halves of each bun with a thin layer of ketchup, then top with a lettuce leaf and a burger. At this point, other burger ingredients can be added, such as gherkins, tomatoes and red onion. Finally, add the top half of the burger bun.

6. Serve with oven chips and some more tomato ketchup, or barbecue dip, on the side.

Sticky tomato and herb ribs

SERVES: 4 | PREP TIME: 1 HOUR, 30 MINUTES | COOKING TIME: 45 MINUTES

INGREDIENTS

1 rack spare ribs

500 ml / 17 ½ fl. oz / 2 cups red wine

2 tbsp olive oil

1 onion, finely chopped

2 cloves of garlic, crushed

1 red chilli (chili), finely chopped

2 tbsp fresh thyme leaves

250 ml / 9 fl. oz / 1 cup tomato passata

2 tbsp coriander (cilantro) leaves, finely chopped

METHOD

1. Cut the rib rack into sections to fit in a large saucepan and pour over the wine and 500 ml of water. Simmer gently for 1 hour, then leave to cool in the cooking liquid.

2. Meanwhile, heat the oil in a sauté pan and fry the onion, garlic, chilli and thyme for 10 minutes over a low heat.

3. Pour in the tomato passata and add a ladleful of the spare rib cooking liquor and simmer for 15 minutes.

4. Stir in the coriander, then transfer the sauce to a liquidizer and blend until smooth. Leave to cool.

5. Drain the ribs and pat dry with kitchen paper. Peel away the tough membrane from the back of the ribs. Brush liberally with the tomato sauce, then refrigerate until you are ready to cook.

6. Cook over a medium barbecue for 20 minutes, basting regularly with tomato sauce, until the glaze is lightly caramelised and the meat is piping hot all through.

Kofta with chips

SERVES: 2-4 | PREP TIME: 15 MINUTES | COOKING TIME: 30 MINUTES

INGREDIENTS

4 large Maris Piper potatoes, chipped

500 g / 1 lb 1 oz lamb mince

2 cloves of garlic, minced

1 shallot, finely chopped

1 egg, beaten

1 tbsp breadcrumbs

1 tsp ground cumin

1 tsp ground coriander (cilantro)

1 tsp paprika

METHOD

1. Preheat a deep fat fryer to 160°C (140°C fan) / 325F / gas 3. Soak wooden skewers in cold water.

2. Place the chipped potatoes into the oil and gently cook for 20 minutes. Remove and leave to cool. Turn the heat on the fryer up to 190°C (170°C fan) / 375F / gas 5.

3. Combine the lamb mince with the remaining ingredients. Using your hands bring the ingredients together and roll into balls.

4. Place the kofta balls onto skewers and flatten a little. Cook on the hot grill for around 25 minutes turning occasionally.

5. Return the chips to the fryer and cook for 2–3 minutes until crisp and golden. Place onto kitchen paper to drain and season.

6. Serve the cooked lamb koftas with the chips, green salad and flat breads.

Beer and chilli baby ribs

SERVES: 4 | PREP TIME: 30 MINUTES | COOKING TIME: 1 HOUR, 20 MINUTES

INGREDIENTS

2 racks baby back ribs, cut in half

1 litre / 1 pint 15 fl. oz / 4 cups beer

175 g / 6 oz / ½ cup chilli jam (chili jelly)

METHOD

1. Put the meat and beer in a pan and simmer gently for 1 hour. Leave to cool in the liquid.

2. Drain the ribs, then pat dry with kitchen paper. Peel away the tough membrane.

3. Brush liberally with chilli jam, then refrigerate until you are ready to cook.

4. Cook over a medium barbecue for 20 minutes, basting regularly with jam, until the glaze is lightly caramelised and the meat is piping hot throughout.

Rosemary chicken with puttanesca sauce

SERVES: 4 | PREP TIME: 15 MINUTES | COOKING TIME: 20 MINUTES

INGREDIENTS

4 skinless chicken breasts

50 ml / 1 ¾ fl. oz / ¼ cup olive oil

2 tbsp fresh rosemary, finely chopped, plus a few sprigs to garnish

2 cloves of garlic, crushed

4 anchovy fillets, finely chopped

1 tsp chilli (chili) flakes

400 g / 14 oz / 2 cups canned cherry tomatoes

2 tbsp capers

50 g / 1 ¾ oz / ⅓ cup pitted black olives

2 tbsp flat leaf parsley, finely chopped

METHOD

1. Cut the chicken breasts in half horizontally with a sharp knife. Brush the chicken with 20 ml of the olive oil and sprinkle with rosemary. Leave to marinate while you make the sauce.

2. Heat the rest of the oil in a sauté pan and fry the garlic, anchovy and chilli for 3 minutes.

3. Add the cherry tomatoes and simmer for 10 minutes. Stir in the capers and olives, then taste and adjust the seasoning.

4. Cook the chicken on a medium-hot barbecue for 3 minutes on each side or until the juices run clear.

5. Add a pool of Puttanesca sauce to four warm plates and sprinkle with parsley. Arrange the chicken on top and garnish with fresh rosemary.

Pulled pork burger

SERVES: 4 | PREP TIME: 30-45 MINUTES
COOKING TIME: 1 HOUR, 15-20 MINUTES

INGREDIENTS

2 tbsp sunflower oil

1 onion, finely chopped

3 cloves of garlic, minced

1 tsp ground cumin

a pinch of ground cinnamon

a pinch of cayenne pepper

100 ml / 3 ½ fl. oz / ½ cup tomato ketchup

100 ml / 3 ½ fl. oz / ½ cup cider vinegar

2 tbsp soft dark brown sugar

450 ml / 16 fl. oz / 2 cups chicken stock

800 g / 1 lb 12 oz piece of pork shoulder,
trimmed and scored

2 large carrots, peeled and shredded

½ small white cabbage, shredded

½ small red cabbage, shredded

110 g / 4 oz / ½ cup plain yogurt

75 g / 3 oz / ⅓ cup mayonnaise

a small handful of flat-leaf parsley, chopped

4 sesame seed buns, split

METHOD

1. Heat the oil in a casserole dish over a moderate heat. When hot, add the onion, garlic and season, then sweat until golden.

2. Add the spices and cook for a further minute before adding the ketchup, vinegar, sugar and chicken stock. Bring to a simmer, stir well, then add the pork and cover. Cook at a steady simmer for 50–60 minutes, then remove from the sauce and pat dry.

3. Preheat the barbecue to a moderately hot temperature.

4. Mix the shredded carrot and cabbages in a bowl. Stir through the yogurt, half the mayonnaise and all of the parsley. Season to taste, then cover and chill until ready to use.

5. Finish the pork on the barbecue for 15–20 minutes, turning frequently.

6. Continue to cook the barbecue sauce in the casserole dish until reduced and thickened.

7. Once the pork is ready, shred it using a fork, then stir it back into the barbecue sauce, leaving to absorb for 10 minutes.

8. Toast the burger buns on the barbecue, then spread the bottom halves with the left over mayonnaise. Top with the pork in its sauce, followed by the coleslaw. Top the buns and serve.

Chicken, beef and chorizo skewers

SERVES: 4 | PREP TIME: 10-15 MINUTES | COOKING TIME: 8-10 MINUTES

INGREDIENTS

2 large skinless chicken breasts

400 g / 14 oz rump steak, trimmed

6 small chorizo sausages

3 tbsp olive oil

½ tsp cumin seeds

a small bunch of thyme, roughly chopped

1 large onion, thickly sliced

METHOD

1. Preheat the barbecue to a moderately hot temperature and soak six wooden skewers in water.

2. Cut the chicken breasts and steak into large chunks and add to a mixing bowl with the chorizo.

3. Add the oil, cumin seeds, thyme, onion and seasoning. Mix everything well until coated, then thread three chorizo sausages each onto two skewers.

4. Thread the chicken pieces onto two wooden skewers and then the steak onto the remaining skewers, along with the slices of onions.

5. Drizzle any remaining oil from the bowl over the skewers, then grill on the barbecue for 8–10 minutes, turning once halfway through cooking.

6. Serve the skewers with pots of salsa and lime wedges on the side.

Beefburger

SERVES: 4 | PREP TIME: **15** MINUTES | COOKING TIME: **10-12** MINUTES

INGREDIENTS

600 g / 1 lb 5 oz / 3 cups steak mince

6 rashers of bacon

100 g / 3 ½ oz / ½ cup mayonnaise

1 tbsp tomato ketchup

a dash of Worcestershire sauce

1 little gem lettuce, leaves separated

4 burger buns, split

1 vine tomato, sliced

1 red onion, thinly sliced

1 tbsp sliced gherkins in vinegar, drained

1 red pepper, sliced

METHOD

1. Preheat the barbecue to a moderately hot temperature.

2. Place the steak mince in a large bowl and add a generous amount of salt and pepper. Mix the seasoning into the mince, breaking it up with your hands.

3. Divide the mince into four and shape into patties between your hands; make a thumb imprint in the centre of each patty before arranging on the rack or trivet.

4. Cook on the barbecue for 10–12 minutes, turning once, until firm yet springy to the touch.

5. Meanwhile, cook the rashers of bacon on the barbecue for around 5–6 minutes until fully cooked and slightly crispy.

6. Whisk together the mayonnaise, ketchup and Worcestershire sauce with a little seasoning for a quick burger sauce.

7. Place a leaf of the gem lettuce on the bottom half of each bun and add a spoonful of the burger sauce, followed by the cooked burgers.

8. Top with a combination of bacon, tomato, red onion, gherkin and red pepper then add the burger bun tops. Serve immediately.

Lime and honey chicken wings

SERVES: 4 | PREP TIME: 10 MINUTES | MARINATING TIME: 2 HOURS
COOKING TIME: 20 MINUTES

INGREDIENTS

2 limes

2 tbsp runny honey

2 tbsp fish sauce

1 tbsp sriracha chilli (chili) sauce

1 clove of garlic, crushed

1 tbsp sesame oil

12 chicken wings, jointed

METHOD

1. Finely grate the zest of one of the limes and set it aside. Squeeze the juice and mix it with the honey, fish sauce, sriracha, garlic and sesame oil.

2. Tip the marinade into a sandwich bag and add the chicken wings. Massage well to coat and leave to marinate in the fridge for 2 hours.

3. Cook the chicken wings over a medium-hot barbecue for 20 minutes, turning occasionally. They are ready when the juices run clear and the skin is nicely charred.

4. Sprinkle the wings with lime zest and cut the other lime into large wedges to serve alongside.

Beer can chicken

SERVES: 4 | PREP TIME: 20-25 MINUTES
COOKING TIME: 1 HOUR, 10-20 MINUTES

INGREDIENTS

1 tbsp smoked paprika

1 tsp golden caster (superfine) sugar

a pinch of ground cumin

2 tbsp sunflower oil

1.5 kg / 3 lb 5 oz chicken, cleaned and trimmed

400 ml / 14 fl. oz can of beer or lager

METHOD

1. Preheat the barbecue to a moderate temperature – around 200°C / 400F. It is important that your barbecue has a lid that will easily cover the chicken when it is cooking upright.

2. Mix together the paprika, sugar, cumin and seasoning to make a dry rub.

3. Add the sunflower oil slowly and stir until you have a paste-like consistency before massaging into the chicken.

4. Open the can of beer and pour half into a glass; lower the cavity of the chicken over and onto the can of beer.

5. Sit the beer can and chicken upright on the barbecue and cover carefully with the lid.

6. Roast the chicken for 1 hour 10–20 minutes until the meat pulls away from the bone and juices run clear when the thickest part of the thigh is pierced.

7. Carefully remove the chicken from the barbecue and cover it loosely with a piece of aluminium foil. Leave to rest for 10 minutes before serving.

Sharing sirloin

SERVES: 2-3 | PREP TIME: 10 MINUTES | MARINATING TIME: 4 HOURS

COOKING TIME: 15 MINUTES

INGREDIENTS

700 g / 1 lb 8 oz well-hung sirloin steak

2 tbsp olive oil

1 dried red chilli (chili), pierced with a knife

1 sprig rosemary

1 clove of garlic, skin left on and squashed

a pinch of rock salt

METHOD

1. Put the steak in a large sandwich bag with the oil, chilli, rosemary and garlic. Marinate in the fridge for 4 hours.

2. Remove the steak from the marinade and pat dry with kitchen paper. Season liberally with rock salt.

3. Prepare the barbecue with the coals on one side and ensure the metal grill is very hot. Cook the steak directly over the coals for 3 minutes on each side, then transfer to the side without coals. Put a small metal bowl of water next to it on the coals side, then cover with a lid and cook for 8 minutes.

4. Transfer the steak to a chopping board and cover with a double layer of foil and a dry tea towel.

5. Leave to rest for 5 minutes before slicing and serving.

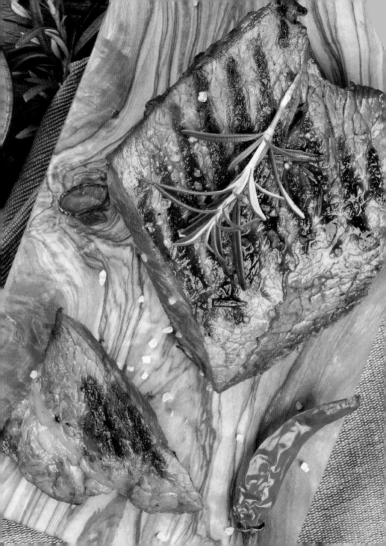

Turkey and vegetable skewers

MAKES: 8 | PREP TIME: 1 HOUR, 30 MINUTES | COOKING TIME: 15 MINUTES

INGREDIENTS

1 turkey breast, cut into 32 chunks

1 large onion, cubed

1 red pepper, cubed

1 green pepper, cubed

2 tbsp olive oil

2 tbsp sundried tomato paste

1 clove of garlic, crushed

1 tbsp lemon juice

METHOD

1. Soak eight wooden skewers in cold water for 20 minutes.

2. Thread the turkey and vegetables onto the skewers and set aside.

3. Mix the oil with the sundried tomato paste, garlic and lemon juice and season with salt and pepper.

4. Thoroughly brush the mixture over the turkey and vegetables and leave to marinate for 1 hour.

5. Cook over a medium-hot barbecue for 15 minutes, turning regularly to ensure the meat is cooked through evenly.

Blackened chicken

SERVES: 4 | PREP TIME: 10 MINUTES | COOKING TIME: 15-17 MINUTES

INGREDIENTS

4 medium chicken breasts, trimmed

2 tsp dried oregano

2 tsp dried thyme

1 tsp onion powder

1 tsp garlic powder

1 tsp smoked paprika

½ tsp cayenne pepper

55 ml / 2 fl. oz / ¼ cup sunflower oil

a small bunch of salad (green) onions, halved

2 green chillies (chilies)

1 small green pepper, finely diced

METHOD

1. Preheat the barbecue to a moderately hot temperature.

2. Cut a few slashes in the chicken breasts and place in a mixing bowl.

3. Whisk together the dried herbs and ground spices with half of the oil until paste-like in consistency; add a little water if it's too dry. Evenly coat the chicken breasts with the paste.

4. Grill the chicken breasts, skin-side down to begin with until blackened, before turning and leaving to finish cooking. The chicken should register at least 74°C / 165F on a meat thermometer.

5. Remove the chicken from the barbecue and leave to rest for 5 minutes, covered loosely with aluminium foil.

6. Drizzle the onions and chillies with the remaining oil; season well, then grill on the barbecue until lightly charred.

7. Serve the chicken alongside the grilled vegetables, garnished with a sprinkle of diced green pepper.

Sweet and sour chicken wings

SERVES: 4 | PREP TIME: 25 MINUTES | COOKING TIME: 14-16 MINUTES

INGREDIENTS

55 g / 2 oz / ¼ cup runny honey

55 ml / 2 fl. oz / ¼ cup distilled vinegar

1 tbsp light soy sauce

2 tbsp sunflower oil

2 tbsp water

a pinch of dried chilli (chili) flakes

900 g / 2 lb chicken wings,
cleaned with tips removed

METHOD

1. Preheat the barbecue to a moderately hot temperature.

2. Whisk together the honey, vinegar, soy sauce, sunflower oil, water, chilli flakes and seasoning until smooth.

3. Add the wings to the marinade and leave for 15 minutes.

4. Shake off any excess marinade, then arrange the wings evenly on the barbecue.

5. Cook for 14–16 minutes, turning frequently, until golden and sticky on the outside.

6. Leave the wings to rest for 5 minutes before serving.

Lamb and beef skewers

SERVES: 4 | PREP TIME: 15 MINUTES | COOKING TIME: 8-10 MINUTES

INGREDIENTS

2 tbsp sunflower oil

2 tbsp water

1 tbsp tomato purée

1 tbsp honey

a dash of Worcestershire sauce

a small handful of basil leaves, finely chopped

450 g / 1 lb lamb neck fillet, trimmed

450 g / 1 lb rump steak, trimmed

METHOD

1. Preheat the barbecue to a moderately hot temperature and soak eight wooden skewers in cold water for 30 minutes.

2. Whisk together the sunflower oil, water, tomato purée, honey, Worcestershire sauce, basil and seasoning in a mixing bowl.

3. Cut the lamb and beef into bite-sized chunks, then add to the marinade. Coat well and leave for 10 minutes.

4. Brush off any excess marinade before threading the meat onto the wooden skewers.

5. Grill on the barbecue for 8–10 minutes, turning once halfway through, until the meat is firm yet slightly springy to the touch.

6. Remove from the barbecue and leave to rest for 5 minutes before serving.

Chicken kebabs

SERVES: 4 | PREP TIME: **35 MINUTES** | COOKING TIME: **10 MINUTES**

INGREDIENTS

2 large skinless chicken breasts, trimmed

2 tbsp sunflower oil

2 tbsp light soy sauce

2 tsp mixed herbs

3 tbsp vegetable stock

METHOD

1. Soak 8 wooden skewers in cold water for 30 minutes.

2. Preheat the barbecue to a medium-high temperature.

3. Cut each chicken breast into four large slices and place in a mixing bowl.

4. Add the sunflower oil, soy sauce, mixed herbs and vegetable stock to the bowl. Mix well to coat and leave for 10 minutes to infuse the chicken.

5. Thread the pieces of chicken onto the wooden skewers and cook on the

6. Barbecue for around 10 minutes, turning once, until the chicken is firm.

7. Serve the kebabs alongside other barbecue meats and sides.

Shallot and thyme smoked sausage

SERVES: 2-3 | PREP TIME: 15 MINUTES | COOKING TIME: 35 MINUTES

INGREDIENTS

2 tbsp runny honey

1 tbsp Dijon mustard

400 g / 14 oz Cumberland ring sausage

2 tbsp butter

3 large shallots, halved

1 large bunch fresh thyme

METHOD

1. Mix the honey with the mustard and brush the mixture over the sausage.

2. Heat the butter in a cast iron oven-proof frying pan and fry the shallots cut side down for 5 minutes over a low heat. Turn them over and scatter over the thyme. Place the sausage on top.

3. Transfer the pan to a medium-hot barbecue and sit a metal bowl of water next to it. Cover with a lid and hot-smoke the sausage for 30–40 minutes or until cooked all the way through.

Glazed duck breast

SERVES: 4 | PREP TIME: 15-20 MINUTES | COOKING TIME: 10-13 MINUTES

INGREDIENTS

4 medium duck breasts, trimmed

75 g / 3 oz / ½ cup orange marmalade

1 orange, juiced

4 figs, quartered

a few sprigs of rosemary, chopped

METHOD

1. Preheat a barbecue to a moderately high temperature.

2. Using a sharp knife, make 5–6 shallow incisions in the skin of the duck breasts.

3. Lay the duck breasts skin-side down on the barbecue and cook over the heat until the fat has rendered away.

4. Mix together the marmalade, orange juice and plenty of seasoning in a small bowl.

5. Once the fat has rendered from the duck breasts and the skin starts to turn golden brown, flip them and brush their tops with the orange glaze.

6. Continue cooking for 5–8 minutes depending on your cooking preference.

7. Remove the duck breasts from the barbecue when ready and leave them to rest on a warm plate, covered loosely with aluminium foil.

8. Place a sauté pan over a medium heat and add a good splash of water along with the figs and a little of the marmalade glaze.

9. Cook the figs until softened, then serve alongside the duck breasts, garnished with rosemary.

Chicken, sausage and vegetable kebabs

MAKES: 6 | PREP TIME: 30 MINUTES | COOKING TIME: 15 MINUTES

INGREDIENTS

1 chicken breast, cut into 12 chunks

3 sausages, quartered

1 red onion, cut into wedges

1 courgette (zucchini), sliced

½ red pepper, cut into chunks

½ yellow pepper, cut into chunks

2 tbsp fresh rosemary, finely chopped,
plus a few sprigs to garnish

1 tbsp pink peppercorns, crushed

2 tsp coriander seeds, crushed

50 ml / 1 ¾ fl. oz / ¼ cup olive oil

METHOD

1. Soak six wooden skewers in cold water for 20 minutes.

2. Thread the chicken, sausage and vegetables onto the skewers and set aside.

3. Mix the rosemary, pink pepper and coriander together then set aside a third of the mixture. Stir the rest into the oil and season with salt and pepper.

4. Brush the kebabs with the spiced oil and cook over a medium-hot barbecue for 15 minutes, turning regularly.

5. Sprinkle the kebabs with the rest of the spice mix and serve immediately, garnished with rosemary.

Grilled pork chops

SERVES: 4 | PREP TIME: 25 MINUTES | COOKING TIME: 10-14 MINUTES

INGREDIENTS

2 limes

2 tbsp sunflower oil

3 tbsp silver tequila

1 ½ tbsp agave nectar

3 tbsp water

4 x 300 g / 10 ½ oz bone-in pork chops, trimmed

a small bunch of flat-leaf parsley, chopped

METHOD

1. Preheat the barbecue to a moderately hot temperature.

2. Juice one of the limes into a mixing bowl before whisking in the sunflower oil, tequila, agave nectar, water and seasoning. Cut the other lime into wedges.

3. Coat the pork chops in the mixture and leave to marinate for 15 minutes.

4. Let the excess marinade drip off the pork chops then grill for 5–7 minutes on both sides until the centre of the chops read 63°C / 145F on a meat thermometer.

5. Remove the chops from the barbecue and leave to rest for 5 minutes before garnishing with chopped parsley and lime wedges.

Chilli oil chicken

SERVES: 4 | PREP TIME: 1 HOUR 10 MINUTES | COOKING TIME: 12 MINUTES

INGREDIENTS

4 skinless chicken breasts

3 tbsp chilli (chili) oil

METHOD

1. Put the chicken breasts between two sheets of clingfilm and bat them out lightly with a rolling pin until they are approximately 1.5cm (½ in) thick. This will help them to cook quickly and evenly on the barbecue.

2. Discard the clingfilm and brush the chicken with chilli oil, then leave to marinate in the fridge for at least 1 hour.

3. Cook the chicken breasts on a medium-hot barbecue for 2 minutes, then turn them 90° and cook for another 2 minutes to make the classic criss-cross pattern.

4. Turn over the chicken breasts and repeat. Pierce the centre of the chicken with a skewer – if the juices run clear, it is ready.

Mediterranean chicken sausages

MAKES: 12 | PREP TIME: 45 MINUTES | MARINATING TIME: 4 HOURS
COOKING TIME: 45 MINUTES

INGREDIENTS

1.2 kg / 2 lb 10 oz / 8 ⅓ cups chicken thigh, chopped

2 cloves of garlic, crushed

2 lemons, zest finely grated

50 g / 1 ¾ oz / ½ cup Parmesan, finely grated

50 g / 1 ¾ oz / ½ cup sundried tomato paste

a small bunch basil, chopped

natural sausage casings

METHOD

1. Put all of the ingredients in a food processor and pulse until finely chopped and evenly mixed.

2. Fill the sausage casings with the mixture using a sausage machine or a large piping bag, ensuring you eliminate any air pockets. Twist into 12 sausages and snip with scissors to separate.

3. Leave the sausages to rest in the fridge for 4 hours.

4. Barbecue the sausages over medium-low coals for 20 minutes, turning regularly. Make sure they are piping hot throughout before serving.

Pork ribs

SERVES: 4 | PREP TIME: 30-45 MINUTES | COOKING TIME: 40-45 MINUTES

INGREDIENTS

55 ml / 2 fl. oz / ¼ cup dark rum

75 g / 3 oz / ⅓ cup Demerara (Turbinado) sugar

75 ml / 3 fl. oz / ⅓ cup dark soy sauce

55 g / 2 oz / ¼ cup runny honey

2 cloves of garlic, minced

1 tbsp Dijon mustard

1 tbsp tomato purée

a pinch of cayenne pepper

freshly ground black pepper

1 kg / 2 lb 4 oz pork spare ribs

METHOD

1. Preheat the barbecue to a moderately hot temperature and preheat the oven to 180°C (160°C fan) / 350F / gas 4 at the same time.

2. Whisk together the rum, sugar, soy sauce, honey, garlic, mustard, tomato purée, cayenne and plenty of black pepper in a small mixing bowl.

3. Pour the sauce over the ribs and massage into them using your hands; leave them to sit for 15 minutes.

4. Brush any excess marinade off the ribs and reserve, then place the ribs on a baking tray; cook in the oven for 30 minutes.

5. Remove the ribs after 30 minutes and brush with the reserved marinade, then finish on the barbecue for 10–15 minutes until sticky and starting to form a crust.

6. Remove them from the barbecue and leave to rest for 10 minutes before slicing and serving.

Shredded barbecued pork buns

MAKES: 12 | PREP TIME: 30 MINUTES | MARINATING TIME: OVERNIGHT

COOKING TIME: 10 HOURS

INGREDIENTS

2 ½ tsp fennel seeds

½ tsp cumin seeds

½ tsp black peppercorns

½ tsp coriander seeds

1 tsp garlic granules

1 tsp dried oregano

50 g / 1 ¾ oz / ¼ cup smoked sea salt

50 g / 1 ¾ oz / ¼ cup soft dark brown sugar

25 g / 1 oz / ⅛ cup granulated sugar

1 tbsp smoked paprika

1 tsp cayenne

2 kg / 4 lb 6 oz pork shoulder, from the collar end

12 burger buns, halved horizontally

12 slices cheese

METHOD

1. Toast the whole spices in a dry pan, then cool. Grind in a spice grinder with the garlic granules, oregano and salt. Mix in the sugars, smoked paprika and cayenne.

2. Rub the mixture into the pork and leave to marinate overnight. Remove from the fridge 2 hours before cooking.

3. Put a pile of charcoal on one side of the barbecue and top it with wood chips. Light a large handful of coals in a chimney starter and burn until the flames die down. Tip them onto the wood chips and place a metal tray of water on the empty side.

4. Fit the grill rack and position the pork over the water tray. Put on the lid and open the top and bottom vents half way. Smoke the pork for 5 hours or until it reaches an internal temperature of 65°C / 150F.

5. Wrap the pork tightly with foil and top up the charcoal if needed. Replace the lid and open the top and bottom vents fully. Cook for 5 hours or until the pork reaches 93°C / 200F. Leave to rest in a warm place for 45 minutes.

6. Pull the pork and add a little barbecue sauce if liked. Add a slice of cheese to each bun and top with pork, then garnish with your choice of coleslaw and pickles.

Grilled Toulouse sausages

SERVES: 4 | PREP TIME: 10 MINUTES | COOKING TIME: 25 MINUTES

INGREDIENTS

110 ml / 4 fl. oz / ½ cup red wine

250 ml / 9 fl. oz / 1 cup beef stock

1 tbsp caster (superfine) sugar

4 large Toulouse sausages

cooked haricot beans, to serve

chopped parsley, to garnish

METHOD

1. Preheat a barbecue to a moderately high temperature.

2. Heat a pan over the hob on a medium-high heat and add the red wine. Let it reduce by half, then add the beef stock and sugar.

3. Bring to a boil, then reduce the heat slightly and add the sausages to the pan.

4. Cook the sausages in the pan for 10 minutes, then remove them from the sauce (which will have flavoured them) and pat dry.

5. Place the sausages on the barbecue and cook for 3-4 minutes on both sides until lightly charred and browned.

6. Serve immediately on a bed of cooked haricot beans and garnished with parsley.

Grilled chicken with lemon and capers

SERVES: 2-4 | PREP TIME: 10 MINUTES | COOKING TIME: 30 MINUTES

INGREDIENTS

50 ml / 1 ¾ fl. oz / ¼ cup olive oil

1 clove of garlic, minced

2 chicken breasts, skinless

1 tbsp capers

2 lemons, juiced

1 tsp caster (superfine) sugar

METHOD

1. Heat a barbecue or griddle to a medium heat.

2. Combine half the oil with the garlic and coat the chicken. Season with salt and black pepper.

3. Place the chicken onto the grill and cook for 12-15 minutes on each side, it will be ready when firm to touch and the juices run clear when the meat is pierced with a knife.

4. As the chicken is cooking, combine the remaining oil in a pan with the capers, lemon juice and sugar.

5. Once the chicken is cooked, bring the caper and lemon sauce to boiling point and pour over the top of the chicken before serving.

Prosciutto wrapped asparagus

SERVES: 2-4 | PREP TIME: 10 MINUTES | COOKING TIME: 10 MINUTES

INGREDIENTS

400 g / 14 oz asparagus, trimmed

200 g / 7 oz prosciutto

1 tsp oil

sea salt flakes

METHOD

1. Heat the barbecue or griddled to a medium heat.

2. Wrap the individual asparagus spears with the slices of ham, leaving the tips showing at the top.

3. Brush the grill with a little oil before placing the wrapped asparagus onto it. Cook for 8-10 minutes turning occasionally until the ham is crisp and asparagus tender.

4. Place onto a serving plate and sprinkle with the sea salt.

Herb encrusted pork ribs

SERVES: 2-4 | PREP TIME: 15 MINUTES | COOKING TIME: 2 HOURS

INGREDIENTS

1 rack of baby back ribs

2 tsp flat leaf parsley, chopped

2 tsp oregano, chopped

2 tsp thyme, chopped

2 tsp dill, chopped

2 tsp rosemary, chopped

1 lemon, juiced

3 cloves of garlic, minced

2 tbsp olive oil

2 tbsp barbecue sauce

METHOD

1. Preheat the barbecue to a medium heat.

2. Trim and prepare the ribs by removing any excess fat.

3. Combine the fresh herbs, lemon, garlic and oil in a bowl.

4. Liberally season the ribs with salt and black pepper before smothering with the marinade, pressing the herbs into the meat with your fingers. Wrap tightly in foil.

5. Place the ribs onto the barbecue inside the foil and cover the barbecue with the lid. Leave to cook inside the foil for about 1 hour and 30 minutes until tender.

6. Remove from the foil and brush with the barbecue sauce. Place back onto the grill and cook for a further 25–30 minutes until charred and blackened.

7. Place onto a board and cut between the bones into individual portions before serving.

Mexican kebabs

SERVES: 4 | PREP TIME: 20 MINUTES | COOKING TIME: 30 MINUTES

INGREDIENTS

4 small tortilla wraps

200 g / 7 oz chicken mince

200 g / 7 oz pork mince

1 egg, beaten

2 tbsp panko breadcrumbs, lightly crushed

1 tsp paprika

1 tsp cumin

1 green chilli (chili), diced

1 clove of garlic, minced

a small bunch of flat leaf parsley, chopped

a handful of coriander (cilantro)

½ red onion, sliced

METHOD

1. Preheat the oven to 200°C (180°C fan) / 400F / gas 6.

2. Turn a muffin tin upside down and place the tortilla wraps into the grooves to form a taco shape. Bake in the oven for 12–15 minutes until crisp and retain the curved shape.

3. Preheat the barbecue to a medium heat and lightly oil the grill.

4. Combine the chicken, pork, egg, breadcrumbs, paprika, cumin, chilli, garlic and parsley in a mixing bowl. Using your hands combine the ingredients and form in to balls, squash them into oval shapes.

5. Pierce the kebabs with skewers and place onto the hot grill. Cook for 8–10 minutes on each side turning once.

6. Place the kebabs into the taco shells with the coriander and sliced onion.

Classic hot dog

SERVES: 4 | PREP TIME: 10 MINUTES | COOKING TIME: 20 MINUTES

INGREDIENTS

4 frankfurter sausages

4 hot dog rolls

2 tbsp American mustard

2 tbsp ketchup

2 large gherkins, sliced

½ red onion, diced

METHOD

1. Heat the barbecue to a medium high heat and lightly oil the grill.

2. Place the frankfurters onto the grill and cook for around 18-20 minutes turning occasionally until the skin has blistered.

3. Cut the rolls in half lengthways and place the cooked sausages inside.

4. Top with the mustard, ketchup, gherkins and onions as desired.

Barbecued chicken wings

SERVES: 4-6 | PREP TIME: 1 HOUR | COOKING TIME: 30 MINUTES

INGREDIENTS

100 g / 3 ½ oz ketchup

2 tbsp honey

1 clove of garlic, minced

2 tbsp Worcestershire sauce

1 tbsp cider vinegar

1 tbsp hot sauce

1 tsp smoked paprika

1 kg chicken wings

1 tsp cayenne

METHOD

1. Start by making the sauce. Place the first seven ingredients into a sauce pan and heat gently until simmering, stirring regularly to combine the ingredients. Once combined and thickened remove from the heat to cool and season with salt and black pepper to taste.

2. Heat the barbecue to a medium high heat and brush the grill with oil.

3. Season the chicken with salt and black pepper and sprinkle over the cayenne. Place onto the grill and cook for 18–20 minutes until tender.

4. Brush the chicken with the BBQ sauce and continue to cook for a further 8–10 minutes until sticky and charred.

Teriyaki pork kebabs

SERVES: 4 | PREP TIME: 4 MINUTES | COOKING TIME: 9 MINUTES

INGREDIENTS

1/2 cup soy sauce

1/4 cup water

2 tablespoons lemon juice

2 tablespoons vegetable oil

2 teaspoons brown sugar

2 garlic cloves, minced

1/2 teaspoon ground ginger

1 pound pork tenderloin, cut into cubes

1 medium zucchini, cut into 1/2 in pieces

1 large sweet red pepper, cut into 1-1/2 in pieces

METHOD

1. In a bowl, combine the soy sauce, water, lemon juice, oil, sugar, garlic and ginger.

2. Pour half into a large bowl. Refrigerate the remaining marinade for basting.

3. Add the pork to the bowl and turn to coat. Cover and refrigerate for 1-4 hours.

4. Drain and discard the marinade. Alternate pork, zucchini and red pepper onto 4 skewers.

5. Grill over medium-hot heat for 3 minutes on each side, then baste with the saved marinade. Continue basting and turning the kebabs for 4-6 minutes. Serve with a side salad of your choice.

68

Asian pork

SERVES: 2-4 | PREP TIME: 15 MINUTES | COOKING TIME: 30 MINUTES

INGREDIENTS

300 g / 10 ½ oz pork loin steaks
1 tsp fish sauce
1 lime, juiced
1 tsp caster (superfine) sugar
1 clove of garlic, minced
1 tsp sesame oil
400 g / 14 oz egg noodles
1 tbsp vegetable oil
1 shallot, diced
1 in piece of root ginger, sliced
2 red chillies (chilies), sliced
a handful of coriander (cilantro), chopped
a handful of fresh mint, roughly chopped
2 tsp chives, chopped

METHOD

1. Preheat the barbecue to a medium high heat.

2. Combine the pork steaks with the fish sauce, lime, sugar, garlic and oil. Toss to coat and leave until needed.

3. Place the pork steaks onto the hot grill and cook for 10-12 minutes on each side until cooked through. Remove and slice into thin strips.

4. Cook the noodles in a pan of boiling water as per the packet instructions.

5. Heat the vegetable oil in a frying pan or wok over a medium high heat and cook the shallot, ginger and chillies for 3–5 minutes until fragrant. Add the pork and noodles to the pan and mix through the spices, before adding the herbs and quickly mixing through.

69

Lime and chilli wings

SERVES: 4-6 | PREP TIME: 15 MINUTES | COOKING TIME: 20 MINUTES

INGREDIENTS

1 kg / 2 lb 3 oz chicken wings

1 tsp chilli (chili) powder

2 red chillies (chilies), diced

1 tbsp honey

3 limes, juice and zest

2 tbsp olive oil

1 tsp garlic powder

METHOD

1. Combine the wings with the chilli powder, chillies, honey, lime, oil and garlic powder. Season and set aside until needed.

2. Heat a barbecue until medium hot, lightly grease the grill with oil.

3. Place the wings onto the hot grill and cook for 18–20 minutes, turning occasionally to ensure even cooking.

4. Serve with wedges of lime and a chilli dipping sauce.

Vietnamese pork sandwich

SERVES: 2 | PREP TIME: 10 MINUTES | COOKING TIME: 20 MINUTES

INGREDIENTS

300 g / 10 ½ oz pork loin steaks

1 tsp fish sauce

1 clove of garlic, minced

2 lemongrass stalks, chopped

1 tsp Chinese five spice

25 g / 1 oz soft brown sugar

1 tbsp coconut oil

2 sub rolls

1 carrots, julienned

a handful of fresh coriander (cilantro)

METHOD

1. Combine the pork in a bowl with the fish sauce, garlic, lemongrass, five spice, sugar and coconut oil. Toss to coat and set aside until needed.

2. Heat a barbecue until hot and lightly oil the grill.

3. Place the pork steaks onto the grill and cook for 18–20 minutes turning occasionally and basting with the leftover marinade.

4. Once cooked, slice the pork into smaller pieces and place into the rolls with the sliced carrots and fresh coriander.

Toasted sausage sandwich

SERVES: 2 | PREP TIME: 10 MINUTES | COOKING TIME: 30 MINUTES

INGREDIENTS

6 pork sausages

75 g / 2 ½ oz / ¾ cup cheddar cheese, grated

50 g / 1 ¾ oz lettuce leaves

4 slices of bread, toasted

METHOD

1. Preheat a barbecue or griddle pan until medium hot.

2. Cook the sausages on the grill for 25 minutes until cooked through.

3. Remove and slice the sausages lengthways.

4. Place the sausages, cheese and lettuce between the toasted bread.

Grilled chicken salad

SERVES: 2 | PREP TIME: 15 MINUTES | COOKING TIME: 30 MINUTES

INGREDIENTS

2 chicken breasts, skinless

2 tbsp olive oil

1 lemon, juiced

50 ml / 1 ¾ fl. oz / ¼ cup white wine vinegar

50 ml / 1 ¾ fl. oz / ¼ cup water

1 tsp sugar

2 watermelon radishes, thinly sliced

1 carrot, thinly sliced

½ cucumber, sliced into ribbons

100 g / 3 ½ oz mixed salad leaves

METHOD

1. Preheat the barbecue to a medium high heat and lightly oil the grill.

2. Combine the chicken, oil and lemon before seasoning. Place the chicken onto the grill and cook for around 20 minutes until charred and the juices run clear when the thickest part of the meat is pierced with a knife.

3. Whisk together the vinegar, water, sugar and a generous pinch of salt until dissolved. Add the radish and carrot and cover so that they are completely submerged. Leave for 15 minutes to pickle.

4. Serve the grilled chicken and pickled carrots and radish with the cucumber and green salad.

73

Steak

SERVES: 4 | PREP TIME: 15-20 MINUTES | COOKING TIME: 8-14 MINUTES

INGREDIENTS

2 x 400 g / 14 oz rib-eye steaks, trimmed

2 tbsp groundnut oil

METHOD

1. Preheat a barbecue to a moderately hot temperature. Tie the steaks securely using butcher's twine to hold their shape. Rub all over with oil and season generously.

2. Grill on the barbecue for 4–7 minutes on each side, depending on your preference.

3. Remove from the barbecue and leave to rest, covered loosely with aluminium foil, for at least 10 minutes before serving.

Greek gyros

SERVES: 4 | PREP TIME: 15 MINUTES | COOKING TIME: 10 MINUTES

INGREDIENTS

4 beef frying steaks

1 tsp paprika

1 tsp garlic granules

2 tbsp olive oil

4 flat breads, warmed

200 g / 7 oz tzatziki

½ cucumber, sliced

2 tomatoes, sliced

½ onion, sliced

1 red pepper, sliced

1 lemon, juiced

METHOD

1. Preheat the barbecue or a griddle pan until hot.

2. Coat the beef with the paprika, garlic, oil and season with salt and black pepper.

3. Cook the steaks on the hot grill for 4–5 minutes on each side. Remove and slice into bite sized pieces.

4. Place the cooked steak into the warmed flat breads with the tzatziki, cucumber, tomatoes, onion and red pepper. Squeeze over a little lemon juice and season to taste.

75

Spicy apple chicken skewers

MAKES: 6 | PREP TIME: 15 MINUTES | MARINATING TIME: 1 HOUR
COOKING TIME: 20 MINUTES

INGREDIENTS

3 skinless chicken breasts

1 red chilli (chili), finely chopped

1 spring onion (scallion), finely chopped

1 tbsp flat leaf parsley, finely chopped

1 clove of garlic, crushed

½ lime, zest finely grated

3 tbsp olive oil

2 apples, peeled, cored and cut into chunks

METHOD

1. Cut each chicken breast into eight cubes.

2. Mix the chilli, spring onion, parsley, garlic and lime zest with the oil and season with salt and pepper. Toss the mixture with the chicken and leave to marinate for at least 1 hour.

3. Meanwhile, soak six wooden skewers in cold water for 20 minutes.

4. Thread the chicken onto the skewers, alternating with the apple chunks.

5. Cook the skewers over a medium-low barbecue for 20 minutes or until cooked through, turning regularly.

Beef ribs in barbecue sauce

SERVES: 4 | PREP TIME: 10-15 MINUTES
COOKING TIME: 1 HOUR, 30 MINUTES-2 HOURS

INGREDIENTS

2 x 600 g / 1 lb 5 oz centre-cut beef ribs, trimmed

3 tbsp sunflower oil

150 g / 5 oz / ⅔ cup tomato ketchup

75 ml / 3 fl. oz / ⅓ cup rice wine vinegar

2 tbsp cider vinegar

75 g / 3 oz / ½ cup dark brown soft sugar

a dash of Worcestershire sauce

½ tsp mustard powder

a pinch of cayenne pepper

METHOD

1. Preheat the barbecue to a moderately low temperature – around 140°C / 275F.

2. Brush the ribs with the sunflower oil and season generously.

3. Arrange the ribs on the barbecue and cook for 1 ½–2 hours until the meat is extremely tender.

4. As the ribs cook, prepare the sauce by mixing together the ketchup, vinegars, sugar, Worcestershire sauce, mustard powder, cayenne and seasoning in a small saucepan.

5. Bring the sauce to the boil, stirring frequently, then reduce to a simmer until thickened. Adjust the seasoning to taste.

6. Ten minutes before the ribs are ready, brush them with the barbecue sauce and continue to cook. Remove the ribs from the barbecue and brush with more sauce before serving with fries.

Cook's Corner

Brilliant Barbecue

Fish dishes

Shrimp and avocado burger

SERVES: 2 | PREP TIME: 10 MINUTES | COOKING TIME: 10 MINUTES

INGREDIENTS

100 g / 3 ½ oz prawns

½ lemon, juiced

1 tsp chilli (chili) flakes

1 tbsp oil

2 burger buns, sliced

1 avocado, sliced

1 tomato, sliced

50 g / 1 ¾ oz rocket (arugula)

2 slices of gruyère cheese

METHOD

1. Heat the barbecue to a medium heat, place a pan onto the grill to heat.

2. Combine the prawns with the lemon and chilli flakes. Season with salt and black pepper.

3. Heat the oil in the pan until hot. Add the prawns and cook for 8–10 minutes until pink and starting to go golden at the edges.

4. Prepare the buns by topping with the avocado, tomato, rocket and cheese.

5. Place the cooked prawns into the buns and serve.

Spicy prawn and avocado toasts

SERVES: 2 | PREP TIME: 10 MINUTES | COOKING TIME: 10 MINUTES

INGREDIENTS

120 g / 4 ¼ oz king prawns
1 tsp paprika
1 tsp cayenne
1 clove of garlic, minced
½ lemon, juiced
1 tsp honey
1 tbsp olive oil
1 avocado, sliced
½ red onion, sliced
lettuce leaves
4 slices of bread, toasted

METHOD

1. Place the prawns into a bowl with the paprika, cayenne, garlic, lemon and honey. Mix to combine the ingredients and coat the prawns. Cover and set aside until needed.

2. Preheat a barbecue until medium hot and lightly oil the grill.

3. Place the prawns onto skewers and cook on the grill for 8–10 minutes turning occasionally to ensure even cooking.

4. Place the cooked prawns, avocado, red onion and lettuce onto the toasted bread and serve.

Roast whole fish

SERVES: 2-4 | PREP TIME: 10 MINUTES | COOKING TIME: 25 MINUTES

INGREDIENTS

1 whole fish such as trout or bass

2 tbsp olive oil

2 clove of garlic, chopped

1 tsp chilli (chili) flakes

1 tomato, sliced

1 lemon, sliced

METHOD

1. Ask your fishmonger to prepare the fish for you, alternatively do this yourself if happy to do so. Wash the fish inside and out and pat dry with kitchen paper.

2. Place the fish into enough foil to completely cover it. Drizzle over the oil and coat with the garlic, chilli and salt and pepper. Place the sliced tomatoes and lemon under and on top of the fish.

3. Preheat a barbecue until medium hot. Cover the fish with the foil to create a parcel and place onto the hot grill.

4. Cook the fish for 20–25 minutes depending on size. The flesh should flake easily once it is ready to serve.

Grilled prawns with red onion mayonnaise

SERVES: 2 | PREP TIME: 10 MINUTES | COOKING TIME: 30 MINUTES

INGREDIENTS

2 red onions, roughly sliced

2 tbsp olive oil

1 tsp red wine vinegar

200 g / 7 oz mayonnaise

120 g / 4 ¼ oz king prawns

½ lemon, juiced

1 clove of garlic, crushed

2 tortilla wraps

METHOD

1. Preheat the oven to 200°C (180°C fan) / 400F / gas 6.

2. Combine the onions, half the oil and vinegar in a bowl and season with salt and black pepper.

3. Place onto a baking tray and roast in the oven for 25-30 minutes until tender and starting to turn golden. Remove and set aside to cool. Mix the roast onions with the mayonnaise and set aside.

4. Preheat the barbecue or griddle pan to a medium heat. Combine the prawns with the remaining oil, lemon and garlic before seasoning. Place onto skewers and cook for 8-10 minutes, turning occasionally.

5. Serve in a tortilla wrap with the mayonnaise.

Cedar planked salmon

SERVES: 6 | PREP TIME: **2 HOURS, 10 MINUTES** | COOKING TIME: **20 MINUTES**

INGREDIENTS

6 portions skinless salmon fillet

3 tbsp maple syrup

1 tbsp Dijon mustard

a few sprigs rosemary

1 lemon, cut into wedges

1 lime, cut into wedges

METHOD

1. Soak two cedar wood planks in warm salted water for 2 hours.

2. Meanwhile, put the salmon in a large sandwich bag with the rest of the ingredients. Seal it up and leave to marinate in the fridge.

3. Set your barbecue up for indirect cooking, so that all of the coals are positioned to one side.

4. Arrange the salmon on the cedar planks with some of the rosemary, lemon and lime from the marinade. Season liberally.

5. Position the planks on the side of the barbecue with no coals, then cover the barbecue and cook for 20 minutes or until the salmon has only just turned opaque in the centre.

86

Prawn and chorizo brochettes

SERVES: 4 | PREP TIME: 15 MINUTES | COOKING TIME: 4 MINUTES

INGREDIENTS

2 limes

110 ml / 4 fl. oz / ½ cup olive oil

1 red chilli (chili), chopped

2 cloves of garlic

1 tsp smoked paprika

8 king prawns

100 g / 3 ½ oz piece of chorizo, peeled

1 tsp sesame seeds

METHOD

1. Preheat the barbecue to a high temperature and soak eight mini wooden brochettes in cold water for 30 minutes.

2. Cut one of the limes in half and set to one side; juice the other. Combine the oil, chilli, garlic, paprika, lime juice and seasoning in a food processor and blitz until smooth.

3. Peel and de-vein the prawns, keeping their tails intact, then cut the chorizo into eight coins. Thread a prawn onto each skewer with a coin of chorizo between the head and tail. Brush with some of the spicy oil and arrange on a grilling tray alongside the lime halves.

4. Grill on the barbecue for 2 minutes on each side. Remove from the grill and garnish with a sprinkling of sesame seeds, serving with the spicy oil and lime halves on the side.

Crab cakes

SERVES: 4 | PREP TIME: 20 MINUTES | COOKING TIME: 4-6 MINUTES

INGREDIENTS

400 g / 14 oz / 2 ⅔ cups canned white crabmeat, drained and picked through for bone

1 small red pepper, very finely diced

a small bunch of dill, finely chopped

1 tbsp mayonnaise

a pinch of cayenne pepper

1 small egg, beaten

125 g / 4 ½ oz / 1 cup breadcrumbs

55 ml / 2 fl. oz / ¼ cup sunflower oil, plus extra for shaping mixed leaf salad, to garnish

METHOD

1. Preheat a barbecue to a moderately hot temperature.

2. In a large mixing bowl, combine the crabmeat with the red pepper, dill, mayonnaise, cayenne pepper, egg, seasoning and a quarter of the breadcrumbs.

3. Mix well until you can take generous spoonfuls of the mixture and shape into eight patties between oiled hands.

4. Place the remaining breadcrumbs in a shallow dish and dip the patties into the breadcrumbs to coat.

5. Drizzle the crab cakes with a little oil, then cook on the barbecue, oiled side down, for 2–3 minutes until golden brown.

6. Lightly oil the uncooked side before flipping and cooking for another 2–3 minutes.

7. Carefully remove the crab cakes from the barbecue and drain on kitchen paper.

8. Serve immediately with the mixed leaf salad on the side.

Planked lemon sea trout

SERVES: 4 | PREP TIME: 2 HOURS, 10 MINUTES | COOKING TIME: 15 MINUTES

INGREDIENTS

600 g / 1 lb 5 oz sea trout fillet,
taken from the thick end

2 tbsp runny honey

salt and pepper

1 lemon, sliced

METHOD

1. Soak a cedar wood plank in warm salted
water for 2 hours.

2. Spread the sea trout with honey and
season with salt and pepper. Top with the
lemon slices.

3. Toast the cedar plank over a medium-hot
barbecue for 4 minutes or until it starts to
smell smoky.

4. Turn over the plank and lay the sea trout on
top, skin side down. Cover the barbecue with
a lid and cook for 15 minutes or until the sea
trout is just opaque in the centre.

Barbecued sardines

SERVES: 4 | PREP TIME: 8 MINUTES | COOKING TIME: 8-10 MINUTES

INGREDIENTS

12 sardine fillets, cleaned and gutted

100 ml / 3 ½ fl. oz / ½ cup olive oil

1 lemon, juiced

4 lemon slices, to garnish

METHOD

1. Preheat a barbecue to a moderately hot temperature.

2. Make diagonal slashes in the skin and flesh of the sardines, then season the insides with sea salt and black pepper.

3. Drizzle the olive oil over and rub well to coat evenly, before seasoning the outsides.

4. Barbecue the sardines for 8–10 minutes, turning once halfway through.

5. Remove the sardines from the barbecue once the flesh is firm and the skin is golden.

6. Drizzle with lemon juice before serving with lemon slices on top.

Prawn and scallop skewers

SERVES: 4 | PREP TIME: 1 HOUR | COOKING TIME: 4 MINUTES

INGREDIENTS

12 raw prawns, peeled with tails left intact

8 scallops, shelled

50 g / 1 ¾ oz / ¼ cup butter, melted

1 clove of garlic, crushed

1 lemon, juiced and zest finely grated

½ tsp ground coriander

2 tbsp fresh coriander (cilantro), finely chopped

METHOD

1. Soak four wooden skewers in cold water for 20 minutes.

2. Thread the prawns and scallops onto the skewers.

3. Mix the butter with the garlic, lemon zest and ground coriander and season with salt and pepper. Brush the mixture over the skewers and leave to marinate for 30 minutes.

4. Cook the skewers over a hot barbecue for 2 minutes on each side or until the prawns and scallops are opaque in the centre and lightly charred on the outside.

5. Drizzle the skewers with lemon juice and serve scattered with chopped coriander.

FISH DISHES

Tuna burger

SERVES: 4 | PREP TIME: 15 MINUTES | COOKING TIME: 6-8 MINUTES

INGREDIENTS

600 g / 1 lb 5 oz tuna steak, chopped

75 g / 3 oz / ¾ cup pecorino, finely grated

a dash of fish sauce

a small bunch of flat-leaf parsley, chopped

2–3 tbsp sunflower oil, plus extra for shaping

1 lemon, cut into wedges

METHOD

1. Preheat the barbecue to a moderately hot temperature.

2. Pulse the chopped tuna steak in a food processor until roughly minced.

3. Add the pecorino, fish sauce, most of the chopped parsley and seasoning. Pulse again 3–4 more times until just incorporated.

4. Remove the mixture from the processor and divide into four, then shape into patties between oiled hands.

5. Cook the tuna patties on the barbecue for 3–4 minutes until lightly charred underneath and starting to release from the grill.

6. Flip and cook the other side for a further 3–4 minutes until the burgers are firm yet slightly springy to the touch.

7. Remove from the barbecue and serve with lemon wedges and more parsley on the side.

Barbecued whole fish

SERVES: 4 | PREP TIME: 15 MINUTES | COOKING TIME: 10-14 MINUTES

INGREDIENTS

4 x 450 g / 1 lb sea bream, gutted and cleaned

110 ml / 4 fl. oz / ½ cup extra virgin olive oil

8 cloves of garlic, finely sliced

1 tbsp red peppercorns

crushed sea salt

METHOD

1. Preheat a barbecue to a moderately hot temperature.

2. Make 4–5 incisions on each side of the skin of the sea bream.

3. Whisk together the olive oil, garlic and peppercorns, then drizzle over the bream, rubbing the mixture into the incisions. Season with the crushed sea salt.

4. Barbecue the bream for 5–7 minutes on one side, then turn and cook for a further 5–7 minutes until the skin is golden and crisp. The thickest part of the fish should read at least 60°C / 140F on a thermometer.

5. Remove the bream from the barbecue and leave to rest for 5 minutes before serving.

Spicy prawn and pineapple skewers

SERVES: 6 | PREP TIME: 1 HOUR | COOKING TIME: 4 MINUTES

INGREDIENTS

18 raw prawns, peeled with tails left intact

400 g / 14 oz / 2 cup canned pineapple chunks in syrup

2 tbsp butter, melted

1 tsp smoked paprika

½ tsp ground cumin

1 tbsp flat leaf parsley, chopped

1 lemon, cut into wedges

METHOD

1. Soak six wooden skewers in cold water for 20 minutes.

2. Thread the prawns and pineapple chunks onto the skewers.

3. Mix 50 ml of the pineapple syrup with the butter, paprika and cumin and season with salt and pepper. Brush the mixture over the skewers and leave to marinate for 30 minutes.

4. Cook the skewers over a hot barbecue for 2 minutes on each side or until the prawns are opaque in the centre and lightly charred on the outside.

5. Sprinkle the skewers with parsley and serve with lemon wedges for squeezing over.

Hot smoked salmon

SERVES: 4 | PREP TIME: 30 MINUTES | CHILLING TIME: 1 HOUR
COOKING TIME: 30 MINUTES

INGREDIENTS

25 g / 1 oz / ⅛ cup sea salt

1 lemon, zest thinly pared, flesh sliced

1 tsp white peppercorns

1 tbsp caster (superfine) sugar

a few sprigs dill

4 portions salmon fillet

METHOD

1. Put the salt, lemon zest, peppercorns and sugar in a saucepan with 250 ml of water. Stir over a low heat until the salt dissolves, then leave to cool.

2. Put the salmon, dill and lemon slices into the brine, then chill for 1 hour.

3. Set your barbecue up for indirect cooking, so that all of the coals are positioned to one side. Place a metal tray of cold water next to the coals.

4. Toast a cedar plank over the hot coals for 4 minutes, then turn it over and position above the water tray.

5. Remove the salmon from the brine and pat dry. Lay the salmon on top of the plank and top with some of the lemon and dill if you like.

6. Cover the barbecue with a lid and hot-smoke the salmon for 25–30 minutes or until the centre has just turned opaque. Garnish with black pepper to taste before serving.

Grilled scallop brochettes

SERVES: 4 | PREP TIME: 45 MINUTES | COOKING TIME: 7-8 MINUTES

INGREDIENTS

1 large lobster tail, peeled and cut into
4 large chunks

½ small pineapple, peeled and cut into
large chunks

8 queen scallops, roe removed

3 tbsp olive oil

2 large vine tomatoes, halved horizontally

a pinch of dried thyme

300 g / 10 ½ oz / 2 ½ cups cooked wild rice, to serve

a small handful of rocket (arugula)
leaves, to garnish

METHOD

1. Preheat the barbecue to a moderately hot temperature and soak four wooden skewers in cold water for 30 minutes.

2. Thread the lobster onto the centre of the wooden skewers, with two chunks of pineapple and then two scallops either side of it.

3. Brush the brochettes with a little olive oil and season generously.

4. Brush the tomato halves with a little oil before adding thyme and seasoning.

5. Grill the brochettes for 5–6 minutes, turning once, until the scallops and lobster are cooked through and firm yet springy to the touch.

6. Remove the brochettes from the barbecue and leave them to rest while you grill the tomato halves for 2 minutes.

7. Serve the brochettes alongside the wild rice, rocket and grilled tomato halves.

Barbecued mackerel

SERVES: 8-12 | PREP TIME: 5 MINUTES | COOKING TIME: 8-10 MINUTES

INGREDIENTS

1 fresh mackerel per person, Horse mackerel or Jack mackerel can also be used if available

2 tbsp olive oil

salt and pepper

METHOD

1. Ensure the fish are gutted and cleaned before cooking.

2. Dry the mackerel thoroughly with kitchen paper, then brush with oil and season liberally with salt and pepper. This will help to prevent them from sticking.

3. Make sure the metal barbecue grill is very hot before adding the mackerel. Cook over medium-hot coals for 4 minutes on each side or until the skin is brown and blistered and the flesh pulls easily away from the bones at the thickest part by the head.

106

King prawns with courgette and tomato

SERVES: 1 | PREP TIME: 5 MINUTES | COOKING TIME: 8 MINUTES

INGREDIENTS

4 raw king prawns (shrimp)

1 courgette (zucchini), sliced

3 small plum tomatoes, halved

4 tbsp olive oil

METHOD

1. Toss the prawns, courgette slices and tomatoes with the oil and season with salt and pepper.

2. Arrange them in an oven-proof frying pan, then sit the pan directly onto the hot barbecue coals.

3. Cook for 5 minutes or until the prawns start to turn opaque and the vegetables turn golden brown. Turn everything over and cook for 3 more minutes.

4. Serve with crusty bread for mopping up the prawn juices.

Grilled squid

SERVES: 4 | PREP TIME: 10 MINUTES | COOKING TIME: 8-10 MINUTES

INGREDIENTS

3 tbsp olive oil

2 large preserved red peppers, drained

2 large shallots, finely sliced

3 cloves of garlic, minced

2 green chillies (chilies), finely chopped

a small handful of flat-leaf parsley, finely chopped

4 squid tubes (thawed if frozen),
cleaned and trimmed

METHOD

1. Preheat the barbecue to a moderately hot temperature.

2. Heat 2 tbsp of the olive oil in a large sauté pan set over a moderate heat until hot.

3. Sweat the red peppers, shallots, garlic and chillies with a little seasoning for 6–7 minutes until softened, stirring occasionally.

4. Stir through the chopped parsley and set to one side.

5. Brush the squid tubes with the rest of the olive oil and season generously.

6. Grill on the barbecue for 2–3 minutes, then flip and top with the sweated vegetable mixture.

7. Continue to cook for a further minute before removing from the barbecue.

8. Serve immediately for best results.

Paella

SERVES: 4 | PREP TIME: 10-15 MINUTES | COOKING TIME: 35-40 MINUTES

INGREDIENTS

4 large king prawns

2 squid tubes, cut into rings (thawed if frozen)

75 ml / 3 fl. oz / ⅓ cup olive oil

1 onion, finely chopped

2 cloves of garlic, finely chopped

1 red pepper, finely diced

300 g / 10 ½ oz / 1 ½ cups paella rice

a pinch of saffron threads

1.25 l / 2 pints 4 fl. oz / 5 cups chicken stock

1 tsp smoked paprika

300 g / 10 ½ oz / 2 cups mussels, cleaned, with beards removed

150 g / 5 oz / 1 cup clams

75 g / 3 oz / ½ cup firm tofu, cubed

55 g / 2 oz / ½ cup frozen peas

2 lemons, cut into wedges

METHOD

1. Preheat the barbecue to hot.

2. Brush the prawns and squid with a little olive oil and season generously.

3. Grill for 2–3 minutes, in batches, until the prawns are pink and the squid is starting to brown.

4. Set to one side while you prepare the paella rice.

5. Heat the rest of the olive oil in a large shallow pan and cook the onion and garlic until softened and starting to brown.

6. Add the red pepper and cook for a further 5 minutes, then stir in the paella rice and coat thoroughly in the oil.

7. Stir the saffron into the stock, then pour it over the rice.

8. Add the paprika, stir, bring to a simmer, then simmer uncovered for 20 minutes.

9. Add the mussels, clams and tofu and cook for a further 8–10 minutes until everything is just cooked through and the mussels have opened; discard any that don't open.

10. Return the squid and prawns to the pan along with the peas and leave to warm through for 5 minutes.

11. Adjust the seasoning to taste before serving with lemon wedges on the side.

Grilled salmon steaks

SERVES: 2 | PREP TIME: 10 MINUTES | COOKING TIME: 6-8 MINUTES

INGREDIENTS

110 ml / 4 fl. oz / ½ cup extra virgin olive oil

1 lemon, juiced and zested

2 tbsp olive oil

4 x 200 g / 7 oz salmon steaks

4 lettuce leaves, to serve

4 cherry tomatoes, sliced in half

1 lemon, thinly sliced

METHOD

1. Preheat a barbecue to a medium temperature.

2. Brush the salmon with olive oil on both sides, then season with salt and pepper.

3. Cook the salmon on the barbecue for 3-4 minutes on each side until fully cooked through and char lines are visible on each side.

4. Divide the salmon between two plates and serve with the lettuce leaves, tomatoes and slices of lemon.

Barbecued swordfish

SERVES: 4 | PREP TIME: 15 MINUTES | COOKING TIME: 12-16 MINUTES

INGREDIENTS

4 x 250 g / 9 oz swordfish steaks

2 tbsp olive oil

2 courgettes (zucchinis), sliced

1 aubergine (eggplant), chopped

1 large onion, chopped

1 yellow pepper, sliced

1 red pepper, sliced

1 lemon, thinly sliced

2 tbsp extra virgin olive oil

a pinch of cayenne pepper

a small handful of pea shoots, to garnish

METHOD

1. Preheat a barbecue to a moderately hot temperature.

2. Brush the swordfish steaks with a little olive oil, then season both sides with salt and pepper.

3. Cook the steaks on the barbecue for 6–8 minutes, turning once halfway through, until they are slightly charred and firm yet springy to the touch.

4. Remove from the barbecue and leave to rest, covered loosely with aluminium foil.

5. Toss the chopped and sliced vegetables and lemon with extra virgin olive oil and a little seasoning, then cook for 6–8 minutes on the barbecue until softened and charred.

6. Pile the swordfish steaks onto plates and top with the vegetables and the lemon.

7. Garnish with a pinch of cayenne and a few pea shoots before serving.

Monkfish kebabs

SERVES: 4 | PREP TIME: 40 MINUTES | COOKING TIME: 5-6 MINUTES

INGREDIENTS

1 tsp ground cumin

1 tsp paprika

2 tbsp sesame seeds

500 g / 1 lb 2 oz / 2 ¼ cups monkfish tail,
diced evenly

50 ml / 2 fl. oz / ¼ cup olive oil

a few sprigs of flat-leaf parsley, to garnish

METHOD

1. Preheat the barbecue to a moderately hot
   temperature and soak four wooden skewers
   in cold water for 30 minutes.

2. Combine the ground spices with salt, pepper
   and sesame seeds in a shallow dish.

3. Toss the monkfish pieces in the olive oil
   until evenly covered.

4. Roll the pieces in the sesame seed mixture,
   then thread carefully onto the
   wooden skewers.

5. Arrange on the barbecue and cook for 5–6
   minutes, turning frequently, until the fish is
   firm yet slightly springy to the touch.

6. Remove and arrange on serving plates;
   garnish with the sprigs of parsley and lime
   wedges before serving.

Cook's Corner

Brilliant Barbecue

Vegetable and side dishes

Grilled avocado with tomato and feta

SERVES: 2-4 | PREP TIME: 10 MINUTES | COOKING TIME: 5 MINUTES

INGREDIENTS

2 avocados

2 tbsp olive oil

50 g / 1 ¾ oz plum tomatoes, diced

50 g / 1 ¾ oz feta cheese, crumbled

½ lemon, juiced

flat leaf parsley, chopped

METHOD

1. Preheat the barbecue or a griddle pan to a medium heat.

2. Cut the avocados in half and remove the stone. Brush with a little oil and place onto the barbecue or griddle. Leave to chargrill for 4–5 minutes without moving, remove using tongs and set aside to cool.

3. Combine the tomatoes and feta in a bowl and drizzle with the remaining oil. Squeeze over the lemon juice and season to taste with salt and black pepper.

4. Spoon the tomato and feta mixture into the avocado. Serve with a pinch of salt and garnished with the chopped parsley.

Sweet potato wedges

SERVES: 4-6 | PREP TIME: 10 MINUTES | COOKING TIME: 30 MINUTES

INGREDIENTS

6 sweet potatoes

2 tbsp olive oil

6 cloves of garlic, lightly crushed

1 tbsp sea salt flakes

METHOD

1. Preheat the barbecue to a medium high heat.

2. Place the potatoes into a pan of salted boiling water and boil for 12–15 minutes until tender. Drain and set aside to cool.

3. Once cool enough to handle, cut the potatoes in half and then into wedges.

4. Heat the oil in a small pan on the barbecue and add the garlic and fry for a couple of minutes until the oil has been flavoured.

5. Toss the wedges in the flavoured oil before placing onto the barbecue grill. Cook for 6–8 minutes until tender and slightly charred.

6. Place onto a serving platter and drizzle with any remaining oil and the garlic. Season with the salt.

121

Stuffed courgettes

SERVES: 2-4 | PREP TIME: 15 MINUTES | COOKING TIME: 40 MINUTES

INGREDIENTS

3 courgettes (zucchini)

1 tbsp olive oil

1 yellow pepper, diced

2 cloves of garlic, chopped

1 tsp chilli (chili) flakes

1 egg, beaten

1 tsp thyme, chopped

2 tbsp breadcrumbs

METHOD

1. Preheat the oven to 200°C (180°C fan) / 400F / gas 6.

2. Place the courgettes into a pan of salted boiling water and cook for 5 minutes until tender. Drain and set aside to cool.

3. Once cool enough to handle, cut the courgettes in half and scoop out the flesh and cut into cubes.

4. Heat the oil in a pan over a medium heat and add the peppers, garlic and courgette. Cook for 8–10 minutes until softened.

5. Place into a bowl and mix with the chilli, egg, thyme and breadcrumbs. Season with salt and black pepper to taste.

6. Place the mixture into the courgette skins and bake in the oven for 20 minutes until golden.

Crispy fried tofu

SERVES: 2-4 | PREP TIME: 30 MINUTES | COOKING TIME: 20 MINUTES

INGREDIENTS

400 g / 14 oz extra firm tofu

1 tbsp sesame oil

1 tbsp soy sauce

½ lime, juiced

1 tbsp vegetable oil

2 tsp sesame seeds

METHOD

1. Preheat the oven to 200°C (180°C fan) / 400F / gas 6.

2. Place the tofu into a clean kitchen towel and place something heavy on top to squeeze out any excess moisture. Remove and cut into cubes.

3. Place the diced tofu into a bowl with the sesame oil, soy and lime juice. Toss to coat and leave to marinade for 30 minutes.

4. Heat the oil in an oven safe frying pan over a medium high heat. Add the tofu and fry for a couple of minutes turning regularly to brown each side.

5. Transfer to the oven and cook for around 15 minutes until crisp and firm.

6. Toss with the sesame seeds and serve as a side to grilled meats and salad.

Grilled vegetable skewers

SERVES: 4-6 | PREP TIME: 20 MINUTES | COOKING TIME: 20 MINUTES

INGREDIENTS

1 courgette (zucchini), sliced

1 red onions, cut into wedges

1 red pepper, diced

1 yellow pepper, diced

50 g / 1 ¾ oz cherry tomatoes

50 g / 1 ¾ oz chestnut mushrooms

2 cloves of garlic, minced

1 tbsp olive oil

1 lemon, juiced

a handful of basil, chopped

METHOD

1. Place some bamboo skewers into cold water to soak for up to an hour before cooking.

2. Heat a barbecue or griddle pan over a medium heat.

3. Add the vegetables to a large mixing bowl. Whisk together the garlic, oil and lemon juice and coat the vegetables with the dressing. Season with salt and black pepper.

4. Place the vegetables onto the skewers before grilling for 18–20 minutes turning occasionally until softened.

5. Place onto a serving plate and scatter with the chopped basil.

Halloumi and sundried tomato burgers

SERVES: 4 | PREP TIME: 2 MINUTES | COOKING TIME: 10 MINUTES

INGREDIENTS

4 veggie burgers
1 tbsp olive oil
12 slices halloumi
4 sesame burger buns, halved horizontally
12 sundried tomatoes in oil, drained
75 ml / 2 ½ fl. oz / ⅓ cup Greek yoghurt
½ clove of garlic, crushed
1 tbsp dill, finely chopped

METHOD

1. Cook the veggie burgers on a moderate heat on each side, according to manufacturer's instructions.

2. After around 5 minutes, heat the halloumi slices 2-3 minutes on each side.

3. Divide the sundried tomatoes between the bun bases. Mix the yoghurt with the garlic and dill and spoon over the top.

4. Add the veggie burgers, then top with the halloumi slices and bun lids. Serve immediately.

125

Grilled marinated tofu

SERVES: 2-4 | PREP TIME: 1 HOUR | COOKING TIME: 15 MINUTES

INGREDIENTS

600 g / 1 lb 3 oz firm tofu

2 tbsp olive oil

1 lime, juiced

1 clove of garlic, minced

1 tsp dried oregano

METHOD

1. Wash and pat dry the tofu before cutting into slices about 2 cm thick.

2. Combine the remaining ingredients in a bowl and whisk together.

3. Add the tofu slices to the marinade and leave for at least an hour.

4. Heat a barbecue to a medium high heat and brush the grill with a little oil.

5. Add the tofu slices and cook for 6-8 minutes on each side until charred and crisp.

Roast tomatoes with avocado

SERVES: 2 | PREP TIME: 15 MINUTES | COOKING TIME: 15 MINUTES

INGREDIENTS

100 g / 3 ½ oz cherry tomatoes, halved

1 tbsp olive oil

2 avocados, mashed

1 lemon, juiced

1 tsp chilli (chili) flakes

4 slices of bread, toasted

METHOD

1. Place the tomatoes into a piece of foil and drizzle over the oil before seasoning with salt and black pepper.

2. Seal the parcel and place onto the coals of a barbecue or into an oven at 180°C (160°C fan) / 350F / gas 4.

3. Roast for 12-15 minutes until softened and charred.

4. Mix the avocado with the lemon juice and chilli flakes and spread onto the toast before topping with the roast tomatoes.

Roast vegetable salad

SERVES: 4-6 | PREP TIME: 20 MINUTES | COOKING TIME: 40 MINUTES

INGREDIENTS

3 sweet potatoes, peeled and cubed

2 courgettes (zucchini), sliced

2 carrots, sliced into batons

2 small onions, quartered

2 tbsp olive oil

250 g / 9 oz greek yogurt

1 lemon

2 tsp flat leaf parsley, chopped

1 avocado, sliced

a handful of fresh coriander (cilantro)

1 tbsp black sesame seeds

METHOD

1. Preheat the oven to 180°C (160°C fan) / 350F / gas 4.

2. Place the sweet potatoes, courgettes and onions into an ovenproof dish and drizzle over the oil and season with salt and black pepper.

3. Roast in the oven for 35–40 minutes until tender and cooked. Remove and place onto kitchen paper to drain any excess oil.

4. Mix the yogurt with the juice from half the lemon and the parsley. Add a pinch of salt and place into a serving bowl.

5. Place the roasted vegetables, yogurt and remaining ingredients onto a serving dish.

Tofu and chickpea salad

SERVES: 2-4 | PREP TIME: 20 MINUTES | COOKING TIME: 20 MINUTES

INGREDIENTS

300 g / 10 ½ oz firm tofu

50 ml / 1 ¾ fl. oz / ¼ cup olive oil

400 g / 14 oz canned chickpeas
(garbanzo beans), drained

2 radishes, thinly sliced

1 eschalon shallot, sliced

1 red pepper, sliced

a handful of cherry tomatoes, quartered

150 g / 5 ¼ oz canned sweetcorn, drained

a handful of flat leaf parsley, chopped

1 lemon, juiced

1 clove of garlic, minced

METHOD

1. Wash and pat dry the tofu before cutting into slices about 2 cm thick.

2. Heat a barbecue to a medium high heat and brush the grill with a little oil. Add the tofu slices and cook for 6–8 minutes on each side until charred and crisp. Set aside and cut into bite sized pieces.

3. Combine the chickpeas, radish, shallot, peppers, tomatoes, sweetcorn and parsley in a large bowl and add the chopped tofu.

4. Whisk together the remaining oil, lemon juice and garlic before seasoning. Pour the oil over the salad and toss to combine and coat before serving.

Grilled vegetables

SERVES: 2-4 | PREP TIME: 15 MINUTES | COOKING TIME: 30 MINUTES

INGREDIENTS

1 courgette (zucchini), sliced

2 carrots, sliced

50 g / 1 ¾ oz chestnut mushrooms

1 red pepper, sliced

2 tomatoes

2 tbsp olive oil

3 cloves of garlic

METHOD

1. Preheat the grill to medium hot.

2. Place the vegetables onto a baking tray and drizzle over the oil and season with salt and black pepper and scatter with the garlic.

3. Place the vegetables under the hot grill and leave to cook for 25–30 minutes, occasionally moving to ensure even cooking.

4. Pour the vegetables and any collected juice into a serving plate.

Grilled halloumi salad

SERVES: 2-4 | PREP TIME: 10 MINUTES | COOKING TIME: 30 MINUTES

INGREDIENTS

200 g / 7 oz baby new potatoes

50 g / 1 ¾ oz green (string) beans, trimmed

250 g / 9 oz halloumi, sliced

200 g / 7 oz iceberg lettuce, sliced

1 lemon, juiced

2 tbsp extra virgin olive oil

a handful of flat leaf parsley, chopped

METHOD

1. Place the potatoes into a pan of salted boiling water and cook for 25–30 minutes until tender. Add the beans for the last 10 minutes. Drain and set aside to cool before slicing in half.

2. Heat a barbecue or griddle pan over a medium high heat. Lightly oil the grill and cook for halloumi slices for 8–10 minutes turning once.

3. Arrange the lettuce, potatoes, beans and halloumi onto a serving plate.

4. Whisk together the lemon and oil and season with salt and black pepper before drizzling over the salad when ready to serve.

131

Grilled pumpkin and beetroot salad

SERVES: 2 | PREP TIME: 20 MINUTES | COOKING TIME: 30 MINUTES

INGREDIENTS

1 pumpkin or squash, sliced

2 beetroots, peeled and sliced

50 ml / 1 ¾ fl. oz / ¼ cup olive oil

120 g / 4 ¼ oz quinoa

50 g / 1 ¾ oz feta cheese, crumbled

25 g / 1 oz / ¼ cup walnuts, chopped

a handful of flat leaf parsley, chopped

1 tsp Dijon mustard

1 lemon, juiced

a clove of garlic, minced

METHOD

1. Preheat the barbecue or a griddle pan to a medium heat.

2. Combine the sliced pumpkin and beetroot with the 2 tbsp of olive oil. Season with salt and black pepper and place onto the grill. Cook for 18–20 minutes turning occasionally until charred and tender.

3. Cook the quinoa as per the packet instructions, drain well and leave to cool.

4. Combine the cooked vegetables with the quinoa, feta, walnuts and chopped parsley and season.

5. Whisk together the remaining oil, mustard, lemon juice and garlic. Season to taste before drizzling over the salad.

Grilled tofu wraps

SERVES: 2-4 | PREP TIME: 20 MINUTES | COOKING TIME: 5 MINUTES

INGREDIENTS

4 tortilla wraps

200 g / 7 oz tofu, sliced

2 carrots, julienned

1 avocado, sliced

75 g / 2 ½ oz baby spinach leaves

½ cucumber, julienned

50 g / 1 ¾ oz / ½ cup Cheddar cheese, grated

METHOD

1. Fill each of the tortilla wraps with the remaining ingredients and season with salt and black pepper, take care not to over fill as it will make it harder to wrap them.

2. Wrap the tortilla into parcels.

3. Preheat a barbecue or griddle pan until hot.

4. Quickly toast the wraps on the hot grill to seal them and melt the cheese.

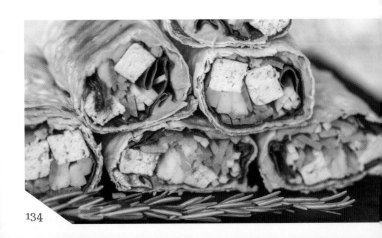

134

Paneer and vegetable skewers

MAKES: 12 | PREP TIME: 30 MINUTES | COOKING TIME: 15 MINUTES

INGREDIENTS

,00 g / 14 oz / 2 cups Paneer cheese, cut into chunks

2 courgettes (zucchini), sliced

2 yellow peppers, cut into chunks

24 cherry tomatoes

75 ml / 2 ½ fl. oz / ⅓ cup sunflower oil

1 large shallot, finely grated

2 cloves of garlic, finely grated

1 tbsp fresh root ginger, finely grated

2 tsp chilli (chili) flakes

¼ fresh coconut, grated

small bunch coriander (cilantro), finely chopped

METHOD

1. Soak 12 wooden skewers in cold water for 20 minutes.

2. Thread the Paneer and vegetables onto the skewers and set aside.

3. Mix the oil with the shallot, garlic, ginger, chilli, coconut and coriander.

4. Spoon half of the mixture over the skewers and leave to marinate for 1 hour.

5. Cook the skewers over a medium-hot barbecue for 15 minutes, turning regularly.

6. Drizzle the kebabs with the rest of the marinade and serve immediately.

Courgettes with chilli gremolata

SERVES: 4 | PREP TIME: 5 MINUTES | COOKING TIME: 8 MINUTES

INGREDIENTS

4 courgettes (zucchini), halved lengthways

2 tbsp olive oil

1 red chilli (chili), finely chopped

2 tbsp flat leaf parsley, finely chopped

1 clove of garlic, finely chopped

1 lemon, zest finely grated

METHOD

1. Brush the courgettes with oil and season with salt and pepper. Cook over a medium-hot barbecue for 4 minutes on each side.

2. Mix the chilli with the parsley, garlic and lemon zest and set aside.

3. Transfer the courgettes to a serving board and garnish with the tomatoes. Sprinkle generously with the chilli gremolata and serve immediately.

Grilled asparagus

SERVES: 4 | PREP TIME: 40 MINUTES | COOKING TIME: 5 MINUTES

INGREDIENTS

350 g / 12 oz / 3 cups asparagus spears,
woody ends removed

55 ml / 2 fl. oz / ¼ cup olive oil

METHOD

1. Preheat the barbecue to a moderately hot
   temperature and soak 6 wooden skewers in
   cold water for 30 minutes.

2. Bunch together four asparagus spears using
   two wooden skewers threaded across and
   through them.

3. Brush the spears with olive oil
   before seasoning.

4. Barbecue for 2–3 minutes on both sides until
   lightly charred and tender.

5. Remove from the grill and serve
   immediately for best results.

Portobello mushroom burgers

SERVES: 4 | PREP TIME: 15 MINUTES | COOKING TIME: 7-8 MINUTES

INGREDIENTS

4 Portobello mushrooms, outer skin peeled away
and stalks removed

2 tbsp olive oil

55 g / 2 oz / ¼ cup mayonnaise

1 red onion, thinly sliced

4 large lettuce leaves

2 slices of cheddar cheese or similar cheese,
thinly sliced

1 large vine tomato, sliced

1 avocado, thinly sliced

4 sesame seed burger buns, halved

METHOD

1. Preheat the barbecue to a medium temperature.

2. Brush each side of the mushrooms with olive oil and season with salt and pepper. Barbecue for 7-8 minutes until cooked through, turning 45 degrees after 4 minutes in order to create the criss-cross char lines.

3. Spread some mayonnaise across the bottom half of the burger bun, then layer on top a slice of red onion, lettuce leaf, slice of cheese, slice of tomato and some slices of avocado.

4. Once cooked, place the Portobello mushroom on top of the avocado and place the top of the burger bun next to it.

5. Serve immediately, with a tomato or barbecue dip.

Garlic and thyme veggie skewers

SERVES: 6 | PREP TIME: 30 MINUTES | COOKING TIME: 15 MINUTES

●●●●●●●●●●●●●●●●●●●●●●●●●●

INGREDIENTS

1 red pepper, cut into chunks
1 green pepper, cut into chunks
1 yellow pepper, cut into chunks
1 red onion, cut into wedges
1 courgette (zucchini), halved and sliced
6 button mushrooms
10 cherry tomatoes
50 g / 1 ¾ oz / ¼ cup butter, softened
2 cloves of garlic, crushed
2 tbsp fresh thyme leaves, plus extra to serve
1 tbsp rosemary leaves, chopped

METHOD

1. Soak six wooden skewers in cold water for 20 minutes.

2. Thread the vegetables onto the skewers and set aside.

3. Mix the butter with the garlic, thyme and rosemary. Season with salt and pepper.

4. Brush the skewers with the butter, then cook over a medium-hot barbecue for 15 minutes, turning regularly.

5. Sprinkle the vegetables with a little more thyme and extra seasoning.

Tofu skewers

SERVES: 4 | PREP TIME: 30-35 MINUTES | COOKING TIME: 7-8 MINUTES

INGREDIENTS

350 g / 12 oz piece of firm tofu,
cut into bite-sized chunks

1 large courgette (zucchini),
halved and cut into half moons

2 medium red peppers, chopped

400 g / 14 oz / 2 cups canned artichoke hearts,
drained and cut into chunks

3 tbsp olive oil

METHOD

1. Preheat the barbecue to a moderately hot
temperature and soak 4 wooden skewers in
cold water for 30 minutes.

2. Thread the tofu, courgette, pepper and
artichoke hearts onto the skewers,
alternating as evenly as possible.

3. Brush with olive oil and season generously.

4. Grill on the barbecue for 7–8 minutes,
turning occasionally until the tofu is golden
and the vegetables are tender.

5. Remove from the grill and leave to cool
slightly before serving.

141

Beanburgers

SERVES: 4 | PREP TIME: 40 MINUTES | COOKING TIME: 12-15 MINUTES

INGREDIENTS

500 g / 1 lb 2 oz / 2 ½ cups canned chickpeas (garbanzo beans), drained

150 g / 5 oz / 2 cups chestnut mushrooms, finely chopped

1 tsp dried mint

1 tsp ground cumin

1 lemon, juiced

2 tbsp sunflower oil

4 sesame seed burger buns, halved

2 tbsp tomato ketchup or barbecue sauce

4 lettuce leaves

METHOD

1. Preheat the barbecue to a medium temperature.

2. Cook the chickpeas in a pan of simmering water for 20 minutes until tender, then drain and mash them with the finely chopped mushrooms, mint, cumin, lemon juice, and some seasoning.

3. Divide the mixture into four balls and shape into burger patties in your hands.

4. Drizzle sunflower oil over the patties then grill for 15 minutes, remembering to flip the burger over after 7 minutes.

5. Remove the cooked burgers from the barbecue and assemble the burgers by spreading the bottom half of the burger bun with tomato ketchup or barbecue sauce then topping this with the lettuce leaf and burger.

6. Finally, sit the top of the burger bun on top and serve.

Barbecued sweet potatoes

SERVES: 4 | PREP TIME: 1 MINUTE | COOKING TIME: 45 MINUTES

INGREDIENTS

4 medium sweet potatoes

METHOD

1. Cut each potato lengthways and cook on the barbecue for 35-45 minutes.

2. Insert a skewer or knife into each one to check if they are ready.

3. Serve with barbecued beans and a dip of your choice, or as a side with a main course.

Vegetable kebabs

SERVES: 4 | PREP TIME: 35 MINUTES | COOKING TIME: 6-7 MINUTES

INGREDIENTS

1 large aubergine (eggplant), chopped

2 medium courgettes (zucchinis), chopped

12 cherry tomatoes

55 ml / 2 fl. oz / ¼ cup olive oil

2 tbsp peanuts, crushed

METHOD

1. Preheat the barbecue to a moderately hot temperature and soak four wooden skewers in cold water for 30 minutes.

2. Thread pieces of aubergine and courgette and two cherry tomatoes onto each skewer, spacing them out.

3. Brush with plenty of olive oil and season generously, then grill on the barbecue for 6–7 minutes, turning occasionally, until softened and lightly charred.

4. Remove from the barbecue and sprinkle with crushed peanuts before serving.

145

Grilled halloumi

SERVES: 4 | PREP TIME: 15 MINUTES | COOKING TIME: 6-8 MINUTES

INGREDIENTS

55 ml / 2 fl. oz / ¼ cup olive oil

2 cloves of garlic

a small bunch of coriander (cilantro)

2 red chillies (chilies), finely chopped

1 lime, juiced and zested

1 tbsp baby capers, drained

100 g / 3 ½ oz / ⅔ cup Kalamata olives, pitted

350 g / 12 oz piece of halloumi, cut into even 2 cm (¾ in) thick slices

METHOD

1. Preheat the barbecue to a moderately hot temperature.

2. Pour the olive oil into a mixing bowl, then mince one clove of garlic and finely slice the other. Finely chop most of the coriander.

3. Add the garlic and chopped coriander to the olive oil along with the chillies, lime juice and zest, baby capers and olives.

4. Stir well and add the slices of halloumi; leave to marinate for 5 minutes, then brush off any excess marinade.

5. Grill the halloumi on the barbecue for 4–5 minutes, turning once, until golden and lightly charred on both sides.

6. Season the halloumi with salt and pepper and serve with the olive marinade spooned over and any remaining coriander on top.

147

Spiced fries

SERVES: 4 | PREP TIME: 20 MINUTES | COOKING TIME: 18-24 MINUTES

INGREDIENTS

1.75 l / 3 pints / 7 cups vegetable oil, for deep frying

1 kg / 2 lb 4 oz / 6 cups floury potatoes
or sweet potatoes

1 tsp salt

½ tsp paprika

½ tsp ground black pepper

½ tsp caster (superfine) sugar

150 g / 5 oz / 1 cup cornflour (cornstarch)

175 ml / 6 fl. oz / ¾ cup sparkling (seltzer) water, cold

150 g / 5 oz / ⅔ cup barbecue sauce

METHOD

1. Preheat the oven to 130°C (110°C fan) / 250F / gas ½.

2. Heat the oil in a large, heavy-based saucepan or in a deep fryer to 190°C / 375F.

3. Peel and cut the potatoes into batons and toss with the salt, paprika, pepper and sugar in a large mixing bowl.

4. Whisk together the cornflour and sparkling water to make a simple batter.

5. Working in batches, dip the potatoes into the batter, letting the excess drip off before deep-frying for 6–8 minutes until golden and crisp.

6. Remove and drain on paper towels, then keep warm in the oven as you fry the remaining potatoes.

7. Serve with barbecue sauce on the side.

148

Smoky black-eyed beans

SERVES: 4 | PREP TIME: 15 MINUTES | COOKING TIME: 30-35 MINUTES

INGREDIENTS

2 tbsp olive oil

75 g / 3 oz / ½ cup smoked bacon, finely chopped

1 large onion, finely chopped

2 sticks of celery, finely chopped

1 large carrot, peeled and finely chopped

salt and freshly ground black pepper

1 tbsp tomato purée

1 tbsp plain (all-purpose) flour

1 bay leaf

600 g / 1 lb 5 oz / 3 cups canned black-eyed beans, drained

500 ml / 18 fl. oz / 2 cups beef stock

METHOD

1. Heat the olive oil in a large casserole dish set over a medium heat until hot.

2. Sauté the bacon for 3–4 minutes before adding the onion, celery and carrot, then sweat with a little salt and pepper for 5–6 minutes until softened.

3. Stir through the tomato purée and flour. Cook for 1 minute, then add the bay leaf, beans and stock.

4. Stir well and bring to the boil, then simmer gently for 30–35 minutes, stirring occasionally, until the beans are soft and the sauce has thickened.

5. Discard the bay leaf and adjust the seasoning to taste before serving.

Corn with thyme butter

SERVES: 4 | PREP TIME: 10 MINUTES | COOKING TIME: 25 MINUTES

INGREDIENTS

4 corn on the cob

1 sprig rosemary

50 g / 1 ¾ oz / ¼ cup butter, softened

1 tbsp fresh thyme leaves

½ tsp dried thyme

½ tsp ground coriander seeds

METHOD

1. Put the corn and rosemary in a pan of boiling water and cook for 12 minutes. Drain well and discard the rosemary.

2. Mix the butter with the fresh and dried thyme and the ground coriander.

3. Brush half of the butter over the corn then cook on a hot barbecue for 10 minutes, turning regularly.

4. Brush the corn with the rest of the herb butter, then sprinkle liberally with salt and pepper before serving.

150

Stuffed barbecued peppers

SERVES: 4 | PREP TIME: 10 MINUTES | COOKING TIME: 20 MINUTES

INGREDIENTS

125 g / 4 ½ oz / 1 cup leftover
cooked vegetables, chopped

1 large egg, beaten

2 tbsp crème fraîche

2 red peppers, halved and seeds removed

2 tsp chopped rosemary

50 g / 1 ¾ oz / ½ cup smoked cheddar, grated

METHOD

1. Mix the vegetables with the egg and crème fraîche and season with a little salt and pepper.

2. Stuff the mixture into the peppers, then sprinkle with rosemary and cheese.

3. Set your barbecue up for indirect cooking, so that all of the coals are positioned to one side. Place a metal tray of cold water on the other side.

4. Insert the grill and position the peppers on the side of the barbecue with no coals.

5. Put the lid on the barbecue and cook for 20 minutes or until the filling has set in the centre.

Spicy celeriac oven chips

SERVES: 4 | PREP TIME: 15 MINUTES | COOKING TIME: 40 MINUTES

INGREDIENTS

1 large celeriac, peeled

4 tbsp sunflower oil

2 tsp smoked paprika

2 tsp garlic powder

2 tsp cracked black pepper

METHOD

1. Preheat the oven to 200°C (180° fan) / 400F / gas 6.

2. Cut the celeriac into 1 cm (½ in) slices, then cut each slice into 1 cm (½ in) wide chips.

3. Boil the chips in water for 5 minutes. Drain well. Leave to steam dry for 2 minutes.

4. Meanwhile, put the sunflower oil in a large roasting tin in the oven to heat for 5 minutes.

5. Mix the paprika with the garlic powder, pepper and a teaspoon of salt. Sprinkle the mixture over the celeriac and toss gently to coat.

6. Tip the chips carefully into the roasting tin and turn to coat in the oil. Roast for 40 minutes, turning every 10 minutes, or until light golden brown and crisp.

152

Barbecued brie with courgettes

SERVES: 4 | PREP TIME: 10 MINUTES | COOKING TIME: 10 MINUTES

INGREDIENTS

2 courgettes (zucchini), sliced lengthways

3 tbsp olive oil

1 small ripe Brie

2 tbsp chilli jam (chili jelly)

fresh basil, to garnish

METHOD

1. Brush the courgette strips with oil and season. Cook the courgettes over a medium-hot barbecue for 1–2 minutes on each side or until nicely marked, then transfer to a hot serving platter.

2. Cook the Brie for 3 minutes on each side or until well-marked, but still holding together.

3. While the Brie is cooking, warm the chilli jam in a small pan over the barbecue.

4. Arrange the Brie in the centre of the platter and drizzle with warm chilli jam. Garnish with basil and serve immediately.

153

Corn on the cob

SERVES: 4 | PREP TIME: 15 MINUTES | COOKING TIME: 12-15 MINUTES

INGREDIENTS

4 corn on the cob (in their husks)

100 g / 3 ½ oz / ½ cup unsalted butter, softened

a small handful of flat-leaf parsley, finely chopped

METHOD

1. Peel away the first couple of layers of husk from the corn and soak the corn in a large bowl of cold water for 15 minutes.

2. Preheat the barbecue to a moderately hot temperature.

3. Mix together the butter, parsley and seasoning in a small bowl, then cover and chill.

4. Once the corn has soaked, remove it from the water and pat dry.

5. Half-peel back the remaining husk from the corn, discarding any silk.

6. Cook on the barbecue, turning occasionally, for 12–15 minutes until lightly browned and tender.

7. Remove from the barbecue and spread with the parsley butter before serving.

Braised black beans

ERVES: 6 | PREP TIME: 5 MINUTES | COOKING TIME: 1 HOUR, 45 MINUTES

INGREDIENTS

2 tbsp olive oil

1 red onion, grated

3 cloves of garlic, crushed

1 tsp ground cumin

1 tsp ground coriander

½ tsp ground cinnamon

2 tsp ground chipotle

500 g / 1 lb 2 oz / 2 ½ cups black turtle beans,
soaked overnight

METHOD

1. Heat the oil in a large saucepan and fry the onion and garlic over a low heat for 10 minutes, stirring regularly.

2. Stir in the spices and cook for 1 minute, then stir in the beans.

3. Add 1 litre of water, then simmer for 1 hour 30 minutes or until the beans are tender but still holding their shape.

4. Drain the beans of any leftover cooking liquid and season with salt and pepper. Serve with blackened or jerk chicken or any Latin American barbecue dishes.

Beetroot and couscous salad

SERVES: 4 | PREP TIME: 5 MINUTES | COOKING TIME: 5 MINUTES

INGREDIENTS

300 g / 10 ½ oz / 1 ¾ cups couscous

150 g / 5 ½ oz / ¾ cup sunblush tomatoes,
plus 3 tbsp of the oil

½ lemon, juiced

½ tsp ground cumin

2 cooked beetroot, halved and sliced

1 handful coriander (cilantro) leaves

METHOD

1. Put the couscous in a heatproof bowl. Pour
    over 300 ml of boiling water then cover and
    leave to steam for 5 minutes.

2. Fluff up the couscous grains with a fork.
    Whisk the sunblush tomato oil with the
    lemon juice, cumin and a big pinch of salt,
    then toss with the couscous.

3. Chop the sunblush tomatoes and fold them
    through the couscous with the beetroot and
    coriander.

4. This recipe is delicious served with grilled
    halloumi.

Rice, quinoa and pepper salad

SERVES: 4 | PREP TIME: 5 MINUTES | COOKING TIME: 30 MINUTES

INGREDIENTS

250 g / 9 oz / 1 ¼ cups jasmine rice

150 g / 5 ½ oz / ¾ cup red quinoa

750 ml / 1 pint 5 ½ fl. oz / 3 cups chicken stock

2 tbsp olive oil

1 red pepper, diced

1 yellow pepper, diced

1 green pepper, diced

200 g / 7 oz / 1 cup canned kidney beans, rinsed and drained

1 small handful curly parsley, chopped

METHOD

1. Put the rice, quinoa and stock in a saucepan. When the stock starts boiling, cover the pan, reduce the heat and simmer gently for 10 minutes. Leave to stand off the heat for 15 minutes, without lifting the lid.

2. Meanwhile, heat the oil in a large sauté pan and sauté the peppers and kidney beans for 5 minutes. Fluff up the rice with a fork, then stir it into the sauté pan with the parsley.

3. Serve the rice warm, or chill and serve the same day as a salad. It makes a great accompaniment for Cajun chicken.

157

Bean salad

SERVES: 4 | PREPARATION TIME: 10 MINUTES

INGREDIENTS

400 g / 14 oz / 2 cups canned cannellini
beans, drained

300 g / 10 ½ oz / 1 ½ cups canned
pinto beans, drained

200 g / 7 oz / 1 cup canned black beans, drained

2 tbsp white wine vinegar

1 tsp Dijon mustard

a pinch of caster (superfine) sugar

110 ml / 4 fl. oz / ½ cup olive oil

a small bunch of coriander (cilantro),
roughly chopped

1 red pepper, diced

METHOD

1. Combine the drained beans in a large
   mixing bowl and toss well.

2. Whisk together the vinegar, mustard and
   sugar with a pinch of seasoning.

3. Whisk in the oil in a slow, steady stream
   until you have a dressing.

4. Add half of the dressing to the beans and
   toss well, then stir through the coriander
   and pepper.

5. Adjust the seasoning to taste and serve with
   more dressing on the side.

158

Tomato, olive and feta salad

SERVES: 4 | PREPARATION TIME: 5 MINUTES

INGREDIENTS

12 medium tomatoes, cut into wedges

200 g / 7 oz / 1 ½ cups Feta cheese, diced

75 g / 2 ½ oz / ½ cup pimento-stuffed green olives

75 g 2 ½ oz / ½ cup pitted black olives

2 large lettuce leaves, torn into small pieces

1 small handful rosemary tops

1 large handful basil leaves

2 tbsp olive oil

METHOD

1. Divide the tomatoes between four bowls and top with the feta, olives, lettuce and herbs.

2. Drizzle with oil and season with salt and pepper.

3. Serve immediately.

159

Potato, feta and spring onion salad

SERVES: 6 | PREPARATION TIME: 20 MINUTES

• •

INGREDIENTS

6 medium potatoes, peeled and cut into chunks

4 red spring onions (scallions), sliced

2 tbsp flat leaf parsley, chopped

½ lemon, juiced and zest finely grated

100 g / 3 ½ oz / ½ cup feta cheese, crumbled

150 ml / 5 ½ fl. oz / ⅔ cup mayonnaise

METHOD

1. Put the potatoes in a large saucepan with a teaspoon of salt and cover with cold water.

2. Bring to the boil, then reduce the heat and simmer for 12 minutes or until tender. Drain well and leave to cool.

3. Stir the spring onions, parsley, lemon, and feta into the mayonnaise. Fold in the potatoes and serve at room temperature.

Beetroot, mozzarella and walnut salad

SERVES: 4 | PREP TIME: 20 MINUTES | COOKING TIME: 30 MINUTES

INGREDIENTS

2 medium candy stripe beetroot

50 g / 1 ¾ oz / 1 ½ cups mixed baby salad leaves

1 ball mozzarella, torn into pieces

8 walnut halves

2 tbsp walnut oil

METHOD

1. Put the unpeeled beetroot in a small saucepan and cover with water. Simmer for 30 minutes or until a skewer slides easily into the centre.

2. Transfer the beetroot to a bowl of iced water and leave to cool. Pull off the stalks and slip off the skins, then thinly slice them with a sharp knife or mandolin.

3. Arrange the salad leaves on a serving plate and top with the beetroot, mozzarella and walnuts. Drizzle with walnut oil and season.

161

Potato salad

SERVES: 4 | PREP TIME: 10 MINUTES | COOKING TIME: 15-20 MINUTES

INGREDIENTS

1 kg / 2 lb 4 oz / 6 ⅔ cups new potatoes

1 large shallot, finely chopped

75 ml / 3 fl. oz / ⅓ cup extra virgin olive oil

½ lemon, juiced

a small bunch of flat-leaf parsley, finely chopped

a small bunch of chervil, finely chopped

METHOD

1. Cook the potatoes in a large saucepan of salted, boiling water for 15–20 minutes until tender to the point of a knife.

2. Drain and leave to cool before cutting larger potatoes in half.

3. Place the potatoes in a bowl and add the shallot, olive oil, lemon juice, parsley, chervil and seasoning.

4. Stir well to combine; serve warm or cold.

Apple coleslaw

SERVES: 4 | PREPARATION TIME: 20 MINUTES

INGREDIENTS

1 small white cabbage

150 g / 5 oz / ⅔ cup plain yogurt

2 tbsp mayonnaise

4 large carrots, peeled

2 apples, cored

1 lemon, juiced

freshly ground black pepper

a pinch of rosemary leaves

METHOD

1. Shred the cabbage using a sharp knife, then place it in a mixing bowl with the yogurt and mayonnaise.

2. Finely slice the carrot and apples then add these to the bowl too.

3. Add the juice of one lemon and mix well to coat the ingredients.

4. Spoon the coleslaw onto a plate or into a bowl and grind some black pepper over the top.

5. Garnish with rosemary leaves, if desired, and serve immediately.

163

Beetroot hummus

SERVES: 4 | PREPARATION TIME: 5 MINUTES

INGREDIENTS

400 g / 14 oz / 2 ⅔ cups canned chickpeas (garbanzo beans), drained

2 cooked beetroot, quartered

6 tbsp olive oil, plus extra for drizzling

1 tbsp tahini paste

1 tsp sesame oil

1 lemon, juiced

1 clove of garlic, crushed

¼ tsp ground cumin

½ tsp black sesame seeds

METHOD

1. Put all of the ingredients, except for the sesame seeds, in a food processor and blend until completely smooth. Add a little cold water to get a creamier texture if needed.

2. Season to taste with salt and pepper, then scrape into a serving bowl.

3. Drizzle with oil and sprinkle with black sesame seeds.

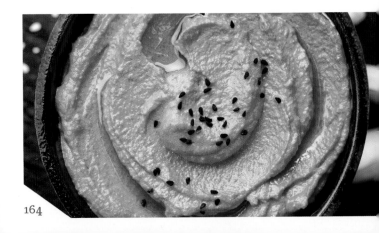

Crunchy winter slaw

SERVES: 6 | PREP TIME: 10 MINUTES | COOKING TIME: 2 MINUTES

INGREDIENTS

1 large carrot, peeled
¼ red cabbage, shredded
¼ savoy cabbage, shredded
½ red onion, thinly sliced
1 small bunch flat leaf parsley, leaves only
2 tbsp pine nuts
1 tbsp pumpkin seeds
1 tbsp sunflower seeds
1 tbsp sesame seeds
1 tsp caster (superfine) sugar
1 lemon, juiced
3 tbsp olive oil

METHOD

1. Shred the carrot with a julienne tool, mandolin or coarse grater and toss with the cabbages, onion and parsley leaves.

2. Toast the pine nuts in a dry pan for a few minutes until golden brown, then add them to the slaw with the rest of the seeds.

3. Stir the caster sugar and half a teaspoon of salt into the lemon juice to dissolve, then whisk in the oil. Pour the dressing all over the salad and toss well.

Salsa verde

MAKES: 150 ML | PREPARATION TIME: 10 MINUTES

INGREDIENTS

2 handfuls flat-leaf parsley leaves

1 handful basil leaves

1 handful mint leaves

1 tbsp capers, drained and rinsed

8 anchovy fillets in oil

1 clove of garlic, crushed

½ lemon, juiced and zest finely grated

3 tbsp olive oil

METHOD

1. Chop the herbs, capers and anchovies together until very fine, then transfer to a bowl.

2. Stir in the garlic, lemon zest, lemon juice and oil, then season to taste with salt and black pepper.

3. Serve as a condiment for lamb chops or fish or use as a marinade for prawns or chicken.

Classic coleslaw

SERVES: 6 | PREPARATION TIME: 20 MINUTES

INGREDIENTS

1 onion, thinly sliced

1 lemon, juiced

2 carrots, peeled

¼ red cabbage, shredded

¼ white cabbage, shredded

1 tsp Dijon mustard

100 ml / 3 ½ fl. oz / ½ cup mayonnaise

METHOD

1. Put the onion in a bowl with the lemon juice and a pinch of salt. Stir well and leave to macerate for 15 minutes to soften the flavour and texture.

2. Shred the carrot with a julienne tool, mandolin or coarse grater and toss with the cabbages and onion.

3. Stir the mustard into the mayonnaise, then mix the dressing with the shredded vegetables.

Sticky pineapple wedges

SERVES: 2-4 | PREP TIME: 15 MINUTES | COOKING TIME: 10 MINUTES

INGREDIENTS

1 pineapple

200 g / 7 oz / ¾ cup demerara sugar

METHOD

1. Preheat the barbecue or a griddled pan/grill to a medium high heat.

2. Cut the top and bottom off the pineapple before slicing into wedges vertically.

3. Remove the woody core of the pineapple and place into a shallow dish. Coat with the sugar ensuring the fruit is covered evenly.

4. Place the pineapple onto the hot barbecue or griddle pan and cook until scorched and blackened before turning.

5. Remove and place onto a serving plate.

Grilled corn

SERVES: 2-4 | PREP TIME: 40 MINUTES | COOKING TIME: 20 MINUTES

INGREDIENTS

2 whole corn with the husks attached

2 tbsp butter, melted

1 tbsp sea salt flakes

1 tsp garlic granules

METHOD

1. Soak the corn in cold water for 30 minutes before cooking. Heat the grill or barbecue to a medium high heat.

2. Combine the butter, salt and garlic.

3. Pull the husk back on the corn and remove the silk. Brush the corn with the melted butter before replacing the husk. This will protect the corn during the cooking.

4. Place the corn onto the hot grill and cook for 12–15 minutes turning occasionally.

5. Carefully remove the husk and return to the grill and cook for a further couple of minutes to add a charred and blackened texture to some of the corn. Serve with extra butter or oil as desired.

Grilled courgette quinoa

SERVES: 2-4 | PREP TIME: 10 MINUTES | COOKING TIME: 20 MINUTES

INGREDIENTS

150 g / 5 ¼ oz quinoa

2 courgettes (zucchini), sliced

2 tbsp olive oil

1 lemon, juiced

2 radishes. Sliced

25 g / 1 oz / ¼ cup almonds, roughly chopped

50 g / 1 ¾ oz pomegranate seeds

basil leaves to garnish

METHOD

1. Cook the quinoa as per the packet instructions, drain well and spread onto a baking tray to steam dry.

2. Preheat a barbecue or griddle pan to a medium high heat.

3. Drizzle the courgette with half the oil and season with salt and black pepper. Place onto the grill and cook for 18-20 minutes until charred and tender.

4. Mix the remaining oil and lemon juice through the quinoa and season to taste.

5. Combine the quinoa, courgette, radish, almond and pomegranate seeds. Toss together before adding to serving plates and garnishing with the basil leaves.

Orange, pomegranate and radicchio salad

SERVES: 2 | PREPARATION TIME: 15 MINUTES

INGREDIENTS

1 orange

50 g / 1 ¾ oz pomegranate seeds

200 g / 7 oz radicchio leaves

2 tbsp olive oil

1 tbsp balsamic vinegar

METHOD

1. Peel the orange and slice off the white pith. Cut into slices removing any pips as you do so.

2. Combine the orange with the pomegranate and radicchio leaves.

3. Whisk together the olive oil and balsamic vinegar and season.

4. Drizzle the dressing over the salad and serve.

171

Griddled aubergine open sandwich

SERVES: 2 | PREP TIME: 20 MINUTES | COOKING TIME: 4-6 MINUTES

INGREDIENTS

2 medium aubergines (eggplants),
chopped into circular slices

1 block of halloumi, chopped into thin slices

6 slices of wholemeal bread

50 ml extra virgin olive oil

a handful of rocket (arugula) or similar
green leaves, washed

METHOD

1. Preheat the barbecue to a medium temperature.

2. Meanwhile, pat the slices of aubergine dry with paper towels to soak up any excess water.

3. Cook the slices of aubergine on the barbecue for 3 minutes until visible char lines appear and they are softened.

4. Meanwhile, place the halloumi slices on the barbecue and allow to cook for just 1 minute on each side until they bubble and turn brown in places.

5. Once cooked, remove the aubergine and halloumi from the barbecue and place two slices of aubergine and 1–2 pieces of halloumi on each slice of bread (three slices per person).

6. Drizzle over the olive oil and garnish with rocket leaves.

Avocado tacos

SERVES: 2 | PREP TIME: 35 MINUTES | COOKING TIME: 10 MINUTES

INGREDIENTS

125g self-raising flour

1 garlic clove, grated

1 lime, zested

½ tsp white pepper

1 tsp ground cumin

200ml water

2 ripe, firm avocados, peeled and quartered

4 corn tortillas

4 tbsp coconut oil

METHOD

1. To make the batter, mix the flour, garlic, lime zest, white pepper, cumin and a pinch of salt in a large bowl. Whisk in the water until you have a smooth batter, then set aside until needed.

2. Heat the coconut oil in a saucepan with high sides. Drop in some batter after a few mins – if it sizzles and turns golden brown quickly, the oil is ready.

3. Grill the avocado for a minute or two until lightly golden and crispy. Remove from the grill and season with salt.

4. Warm the tortillas on both sides for 1-2 mins in a griddle or non-stick frying pan, then add the avocado. Serve with salad and dip.

Grilled vegetable and halloumi burgers

SERVES: 2 | PREP TIME: 5 MINUTES | COOKING TIME: 10 MINUTES

INGREDIENTS

250 g / 9 oz halloumi, sliced
1 courgette (zucchini), sliced
1 aubergine, sliced
½ red onion, chopped
a handful of Romaine lettuce
2 burger buns

METHOD

1. Heat the vegetables for 2-3 mins each side on the barbecue (moderate heat).

2. Meanwhile, grill the halloumi for the same amount of time.

3. Lightly toast the buns.

4. Add all the grilled vegetable and halloumi, along with the lettuce, to the buns and serve with dressing or mayonnaise.

Grilled new potatoes

SERVES: 6-8 | PREP TIME: 10 MINUTES | COOKING TIME: 40 MINUTES

INGREDIENTS

800 g / 1 lb 12 oz new potatoes

2 tbsp olive oil

1 tsp chilli (chili) flakes

2 cloves of garlic, finely chopped

2 tsp rosemary, chopped

METHOD

1. Preheat the barbecue to a medium heat.

2. Place the potatoes into a pan of salted boiling water and cook for 12–15 minutes until softened. Drain and place into a bowl.

3. Place the remaining ingredients into the bowl with the potatoes and toss to coat.

4. Place the potatoes onto skewers and place over the hot coals. Cook for 20–25 minutes until charred and tender.

Italian grilled courgettes

SERVES: 4 | PREP TIME: 5 MINUTES | COOKING TIME: 30 MINUTES

INGREDIENTS

4 courgettes

3 tbsp olive oil

½ lemon

a handful of pine nuts

1 clove garlic, finely chopped

parmesan, finely grated

a handful of basil leaves, roughly torn

mint to garnish

METHOD

1. Heat the barbecue to high. Cut each courgette lengthways into 4 strips, depending on width. Season and rub both sides of each slice with a little olive oil and a squeeze of lemon juice.

2. Cook for 5-6 minutes on each side. Transfer them to a serving dish and squeeze over a little more lemon juice.

3. Meanwhile, toast the pine nuts in a pan for 2 minutes until golden. Cover the courgettes with the pine nuts, garlic, parmesan, basil and mint. Trickle over the remaining oil, and toss lightly.

Baked sweet potato

SERVES: 2-4 | PREP TIME: 10 MINUTES | COOKING TIME: 1 HOUR

INGREDIENTS

4 sweet potatoes

2 tbsp olive oil

50 g / 1 ¾ oz cherry tomatoes, halved

300 g / 10 ½ oz cottage cheese

METHOD

1. Preheat the oven to 220°C (200°C fan) / 425F / gas 7.

2. Halve the sweet potatoes and place into an ovenproof dish. Drizzle over the oil and season with salt and black pepper.

3. Place the potatoes into the oven and roast for up to an hour until soft. Place the tomatoes into the oven with the potatoes for the last 5 minutes.

4. Serve the potatoes with a topping of cottage cheese and the roast tomatoes.

Grilled fennel

SERVES: 4 | PREP TIME: 10 MINUTES | COOKING TIME: 10 MINUTES

INGREDIENTS

2 fennel bulbs, sliced lengthways
into 1cm-thick pieces

1½ tbsp olive oil

2 tbsp finely chopped black Kalamata olive

1 garlic clove, crushed

juice of 1 lemon

Parsley and basil to garnish, finely chopped

METHOD

1. Heat a the barbecue to a moderate heat. Toss the fennel in 1 tbsp of the oil, coating well. Cook for 5 mins on each side until golden brown and charred.

2. For the dressing, put the olives, garlic, lemon juice and remaining oil in a bowl. Add the chopped herbs and combine.

3. Lay the fennel on a platter and add the dressing.

Barbecued watermelon salad

SERVES: 4 | PREP TIME: 4 MINUTES | COOKING TIME: 4 MINUTES

INGREDIENTS

4 wedges watermelon, peeled and sliced

75 g / 2 ½ / 2 ¼ cups mixed baby salad leaves

150 g / 5 ½ oz / 1 cup mini mozzarella, drained

2 tbsp olive oil

1 lime, juiced

METHOD

1. Cook the watermelon pieces over a hot barbecue for 2 minutes on each side or until nicely charred.

2. Arrange the salad leaves on four plates and top with the mozzarella and watermelon.

3. Drizzle the salad with oil and lime juice and season with salt and pepper just before serving.

Mango pickle

SERVES: 6-8 | PREPARATION TIME: 1 DAY

INGREDIENTS

2 mangoes

1 tbsp mustard seeds

1 tsp fenugreek seeds

1 tsp chilli (chili) flakes

2 tbsp red chilli (chili) powder

4 cloves of garlic, crushed

25 ml / ¾ fl. oz sesame oil

1 tbsp sea salt

METHOD

1. For this recipe choose unripe mangoes that are still firm.

2. Chop the mango into cubes and place into a bowl.

3. Toast the seeds in a dry pan and lightly crush in a pestle and mortar with the chilli flakes.

4. Add the toasted seeds, chilli powder, garlic, oil and salt to the mango. Mix to combine, cover and leave for 24 hours.

5. Check taste and season if required. Place into a clean jar, this will keep up to 10 days in the refrigerator.

181

Grilled peppers

SERVES: 2 -4 | PREP TIME: 5 MINUTES | COOKING TIME: 15 MINUTES

INGREDIENTS

6 peppers

2 tbsp olive oil

sea salt

METHOD

1. Preheat the barbecue or griddle pan to a medium high heat.

2. Coat the peppers with the oil and a pinch of salt.

3. Grill the peppers for 12-15 minutes turning occasionally until the skin has blistered and blackened.

4. Remove from the pan and either serve hot with grilled meats or allow to cool and add to a salad.

Tomato salsa

SERVES: 4 | PREPARATION TIME: 40 MINUTES

INGREDIENTS

½ small red onion, roughly chopped

a small bunch of coriander (cilantro),
roughly chopped

1 lime, juiced

1 tbsp distilled vinegar

a pinch of caster (superfine) sugar

400 g / 14 oz / 2 cups canned chopped tomatoes

salt and freshly ground black pepper

METHOD

1. In a food processor, pulse together the red onion, coriander, lime juice, vinegar, sugar and a little seasoning until the onion and coriander are finely chopped.

2. Add the tomatoes and pulse again until you have a smoother salsa that still has a little texture.

3. Adjust the seasoning to taste, then cover and chill for 30 minutes.

4. Serve chilled.

183

Barbecue sauce

SERVES: 4-6 | PREP TIME: 10 MINUTES | COOKING TIME: 20-25 MINUTES

INGREDIENTS

1 tbsp sunflower oil

2 cloves of garlic, minced

200 g / 7 oz / 1 cup passata

3 tbsp distilled vinegar

85 g / 3 ½ oz / ½ cup soft dark brown sugar

3 tbsp Worcestershire sauce

METHOD

1. Heat the oil in a saucepan over a medium-high heat until it is hot.

2. Add the garlic and cook for 5 minutes, stirring occasionally to avoid burning, until soft and golden. Add the passata, vinegar, sugar and Worcestershire sauce. Stir well then bring to the boil.

3. Once the mixture has boiled for 30 seconds, reduce the heat and simmer gently for 20 minutes until completely thickened, stirring occasionally.

4. Season to taste with salt and pepper then spoon into a dip bowl to serve.

Mayonnaise

MAKES: 500 G | PREPARATION TIME: 40 MINUTES

INGREDIENTS

2 large egg yolks (as fresh as possible)

1 tsp Dijon mustard

salt and ground white pepper

475 ml / 17 fl. oz / 2 cups sunflower oil

1–2 tbsp white wine vinegar

METHOD

1. Whisk the egg yolks and mustard together in a large mixing bowl.

2. Add a little seasoning and whisk again briefly.

3. Gradually whisk in the oil, drip by drip, for 3–4 minutes until a thick mixture takes shape.

4. After half of the oil has been incorporated, add the white wine vinegar to taste.

5. Continue to whisk in the rest of the oil in a slow, steady stream. Adjust the seasoning to taste.

6. Cover and chill the mayonnaise for up to one week.

Guacamole

SERVES: 4 | PREPARATION TIME: 10 MINUTES

INGREDIENTS

½ red onion, finely chopped

2 cloves of garlic, roughly chopped

1 lime, juiced

1 tbsp olive oil

a dash of hot sauce

2 large, ripe Hass avocados, halved, peeled and roughly chopped

METHOD

1. In a food processor, blitz the onion, garlic, lime juice, olive oil, hot sauce and one of the avocados until smooth.

2. Add the remaining avocado and blitz again until smooth.

3. Adjust the seasoning to taste before serving with tortilla chips for dipping.

Chilli and thyme finishing salt

MAKES: 75 G | PREP TIME: 10 MINUTES

INGREDIENTS

2 tsp black peppercorns

2 tbsp fresh thyme leaves

50 g / 1 ¾ oz / ¼ cup sea salt crystals

2 birdseye chillies (chilies), thinly sliced

1 lemon, zest finely grated

½ tsp smoked paprika

METHOD

1. Crush the peppercorns with a pestle and mortar, then add the thyme and bruise lightly to release the fragrance.

2. Stir in the rest of the ingredients and then transfer to a small jar.

3. Sprinkle on top of barbecued poultry or fish just before serving.

Spicy barbecue sauce

MAKES: 600 ML | PREP TIME: 25 MINUTES | COOKING TIME: 40 MINUTES

INGREDIENTS

2 chipotle chillies

3 tbsp olive oil

1 onion, finely chopped

4 cloves of garlic, crushed

2 tbsp fresh root ginger, finely chopped

100 ml / 3 ½ fl. oz / ½ cup pineapple juice

100 ml / 3 ½ fl. oz / ½ cup cider vinegar

100 ml / 3 ½ fl. oz / ½ cup maple syrup

100 ml / 3 ½ fl. oz / ½ cup American style mustard

100 ml / 3 ½ fl. oz / ½ cup molasses

100 ml / 3 ½ fl. oz / ½ cup mango chutney

400 g / 14 oz / 2 cups canned tomatoes, chopped

METHOD

1. Soak the chipotles in warm water for 20 minutes, then drain well. Remove the stalks and seeds and roughly chop.

2. Heat the oil in a large saucepan and fry the onion and garlic over a low heat for 10 minutes.

3. Stir in the rest of the ingredients plus the chopped chipotles and simmer gently for 30 minutes.

4. Transfer the sauce to a liquidizer and blend until smooth. Leave to cool completely.

5. Use the sauce as a marinade and glaze for ribs, stir into pulled pork or use as a condiment for burgers and chicken.

188

Spicy rub for steaks

MAKES: 50 G | PREP TIME: 5 MINUTES | COOKING TIME: 1 MINUTE

INGREDIENTS

1 tsp black peppercorns

1 tsp white peppercorns

1 tsp chilli (chili) flakes

1 tsp smoked paprika

1 tsp dried rosemary

1 tsp dried thyme

1 tsp coriander seeds

2 tbsp sea salt

METHOD

1. Put all of the ingredients except for the salt in a spice grinder and whizz until roughly ground.

2. Add the salt and whizz again, then tip into an airtight pot and screw on the lid.

3. Use a level teaspoon of rub per steak, rub it in well and leave to marinade for at least 1 hour.

4. You can also add a pinch of rub to softened butter and turn it into butter pats to melt on top of cooked steaks.

Chilli and garlic butter for shellfish

MAKES: 100 G | PREP TIME: 5 MINUTES | COOKING TIME: 1 HOUR

INGREDIENTS

75 g / 2 ½ oz / ⅓ cup butter, softened

2 tbsp brown crab meat

2 red chillies (chilies), finely chopped

2 cloves of garlic, crushed

2 tbsp French tarragon, finely chopped

1 tbsp flat leaf parsley, finely chopped

METHOD

1. Put all of the ingredients in a bowl with a good grind of black pepper and beat with a spoon to mix.

2. Spread the butter onto halved lobsters, langoustines or king prawns before cooking or add a small spoonful to scallops or oysters cooked in the half-shell.

Blue cheese and chive butter for steak

MAKES: 150 G | PREP TIME: 5 MINUTES | COOKING TIME: 1 HOUR

INGREDIENTS

75 g / 2 ½ oz / ⅓ cup butter, softened

75 g / 2 ½ oz / ⅓ cup Roquefort

2 tbsp chives, chopped

METHOD

1. Beat all of the ingredients together in a bowl.

2. Scrape the mixture into the centre of a sheet of greaseproof paper and shape into a large butter pat. Wrap the butter in the paper and chill for at least 1 hour.

3. Slice the butter and melt onto hot steak just before serving.

Jerk marinade

SERVES: 4 | PREP TIME: 10 MINUTES | COOKING TIME: 4 HOURS

INGREDIENTS

1 tsp sea salt

1 red onion, roughly chopped

1 tbsp root ginger, roughly chopped

2 cloves of garlic, roughly chopped

2 red chillies (chilies), roughly chopped

1 tbsp ground allspice

1 tbsp thyme leaves

1 tbsp dark brown sugar

2 tbsp dark soy sauce

2 tbsp lime juice

2 tbsp orange juice

METHOD

1. Put all of the ingredients in a food processor and blend to a smooth paste.

2. Scrape the marinade into a large sandwich bag, then add your chicken or pork and massage well to coat.

3. Seal up the bag then transfer to the fridge and leave to marinate for at least 4 hours or overnight.

4. If using bone-in chicken, cook over a medium-low barbecue for 35 minutes, turning regularly, until it is cooked all the way through. It's ready when the juices run clear or when the centre reaches 74°C / 165F on a food thermometer.

193

Cook's Corner

Brilliant Barbecue

Desserts

Homemade ice cream

SERVES: 4-6 | PREP TIME: 30 MINUTES
FREEZING TIME: 4 HOURS OR OVERNIGHT

INGREDIENTS

4 egg yolks

200 g / 7 oz / ¾ cup caster (superfine) sugar

2 vanilla pods

500 ml / 17 fl. oz / 2 cups double (heavy) cream

75 g / 2 ½ oz plain chocolate, broken into pieces

METHOD

1. Whisk the egg yolks and sugar together until pale and creamy. Halve the vanilla pods and scrape out the seeds.

2. Place the vanilla pods and cream into a saucepan and gently heat until just starting to bubble. Remove the vanilla pods from the cream and slowly pour over the egg yolks whilst whisking continuously.

3. Pour through a sieve back into the saucepan and add the vanilla seeds. Cover and leave to cool completely. If making chocolate ice cream, add at this stage and warm the mixture just enough to melt the chocolate before leaving to cool.

4. Pour the cooled mixture into a solid container and place into the freezer for 4 hours or overnight until frozen solid.

Grilled pineapple

SERVES: 4 | PREP TIME: 15 MINUTES | COOKING TIME: 3-4 MINUTES

INGREDIENTS

110 g / 4 oz / ½ cup runny honey

1 vanilla pod, split lengthwise

1 large pineapple, peeled and cored

1 lime, juiced

METHOD

1. Preheat the barbecue to a moderately hot temperature.

2. Combine the honey and vanilla pod in a small saucepan and warm over a gentle heat.

3. Place the pineapple on its side on a chopping board and cut into rings approximately 2 cm (¾ inches) thick.

4. Brush the slices of pineapple with the warmed honey, then grill on the barbecue for 3-4 minutes, turning halfway through cooking.

5. Remove the pineapple from the barbecue and drizzle with a little more honey and some lime juice before serving.

Barbecued bananas

SERVES: 6 | PREP TIME: 5 MINUTES | COOKING TIME: 15 MINUTES

INGREDIENTS

12 small bananas
(Lady Finger bananas are ideal)

METHOD

1. Cut a slit down the length of each banana to prevent the skins from bursting.

2. Cook the bananas over a medium-low barbecue for 15 minutes or until the skins are charred and crisp, turning occasionally.

3. Delicious served hot with coconut ice cream.

Toasted marshmallows

SERVES: 4 | PREP TIME: 35 MINUTES | COOKING TIME: 5 MINUTES

INGREDIENTS

150 g / 5 oz / 3 cups assorted marshmallows

225 g / 8 oz / 1 ½ cups strawberries

METHOD

1. Preheat the barbecue to a moderately hot temperature and soak 4 wooden skewers in cold water for 30 minutes.

2. Alternately thread the marshmallows and strawberries onto the wooden skewers.

3. Toast the marshmallows by holding them just off the surface of the barbecue, turning the skewers to evenly toast.

4. Allow to cool slightly before serving.

5. Delicious served with melted chocolate.

Vanilla glazed fruit kebabs

SERVES: 8 | PREP TIME: 30 MINUTES | COOKING TIME: 10 MINUTES

INGREDIENTS

1 star fruit, thickly sliced

2 slices fresh pineapple, cut into wedges

1 banana, sliced with skin left on

1 kiwi fruit, halved and thickly sliced

½ papaya, cut into large chunks

1 pear, halved and thickly sliced

8 strawberries

50 g / 1 ¾ oz / ¼ cup butter

2 tbsp maple syrup

1 vanilla pod, halved lengthways

2 tbsp mixed seeds

METHOD

1. Soak eight wooden skewers in cold water for 20 minutes.

2. Thread the fruit onto the skewers and set aside.

3. Put the butter and maple syrup in a small saucepan. Scrape the seeds from the vanilla pod and add them to the pan, then warm it gently until the butter melts.

4. Brush half the vanilla glaze over the kebabs, then cook them over a medium-hot barbecue for 4 minutes on each side.

5. Brush the kebabs with the rest of the vanilla glaze and sprinkle with seeds.

Pineapple with lemon balm

SERVES: 4 | PREP TIME: 10 MINUTES | COOKING TIME: 4 MINUTES

INGREDIENTS

1 bunch lemon balm

125 ml / 4 ½ fl. oz / ½ cup runny honey

1 pineapple, peeled, cored and sliced

METHOD

1. Reserve a few lemon balm leaves and put the rest in a small saucepan with the honey. Heat gently for 5 minutes to infuse the honey, then strain it through a sieve into a bowl.

2. Brush the pineapple slices with half of the infused honey.

3. Cook the pineapple over a hot barbecue for 2 minutes on each side or until nicely browned.

4. Brush with the rest of the honey and serve hot, garnished with the reserved lemon balm leaves.

Pineapple skewers

SERVES: 4 | PREP TIME: 5 MINUTES | COOKING TIME: 10 MINUTES

INGREDIENTS

1 whole pineapple
1/2 cup freshly squeezed lime juice
1 tbsp brown sugar

METHOD

1. Preheat the grill on high. Peel and remove the core from the pineapple.

2. Cut the pineapple lengthways, and remove any prickly parts.

3. Thread the pieces of pineapple onto the skewers lengthwise. Add the lime juice and sugar, before grilling on all sides until golden brown, approximately 4-5 minutes per side.

Baked banana

SERVES: 4 | PREP TIME: 10-15 MINUTES | COOKING TIME: 10 MINUTES

INGREDIENTS

4 ripe bananas, chopped in half lengthways

3 tbsp runny honey

100 g / 3 ½ oz / ½ cup vanilla ice cream

2 tbsp walnuts, chopped

caramel sauce, to serve

METHOD

1. Preheat the barbecue to a moderately heat. Peel the bananas and brush them with runny honey, then wrap two halves of banana in a sheet of aluminium foil. You will have four parcels in total, containing two halves each.

2. Seal the foil then cook the bananas on the barbecue for 10 minutes until golden and warm.

3. Remove the bananas from the barbecue and let them cool to one side, still encased in the foil.

4. Meanwhile, remove the vanilla ice cream from the freezer and warm for a couple of minutes.

5. Unwrap the bananas from the foil.

6. Arrange two halves of banana on each plate, then place two scoops of vanilla ice cream next to the halves, along with a generous sprinkle of chopped walnuts and a drizzle of caramel sauce.

204

Fruit skewers

MAKES: 4 | PREP TIME: 25 MINUTES | COOKING TIME: 4 MINUTES

INGREDIENTS

8 strawberries

8 marshmallows

1 small melon

1 small pineapple

METHOD

1. Soak four wooden skewers in cold water for 20 minutes.

2. Cut up the melon and pineapple into chunks, ensuring all skin is removed, and remove the tops of the strawberries.

3. Thread the fruit and marshmallows onto the skewers.

4. Barbecue the skewers over the last embers of the fire at the end of the meal for 4 minutes, turning regularly.

Cookie ice cream sandwich

SERVES: 4 | PREP TIME: 30 MINUTES | COOKING TIME: 15 MINUTES

INGREDIENTS

100 g / 3 ½ oz / ½ cup unsalted butter

100 g / 3 ½ oz / ½ cup soft brown sugar

1 large free-range egg

½ tsp vanilla extract

200 g / 7 oz / 1 ⅓ cups self-raising flour

100 g / 3 ½ oz / ⅔ cups plain chocolate chips

300 ml / 10 fl. oz vanilla ice cream

METHOD

1. Preheat the oven to 180°C (160°C fan) / 350F / gas 4 and grease and line two baking trays.

2. In a large mixing bowl, cream together the butter and sugar until light and fluffy.

3. Mix the egg and vanilla extract into the butter.

4. Sift the flour into the butter mixture and fold through before stirring in the chocolate chips.

5. Roll the dough into a thick sausage shape and wrap in cling film. Place into the refrigerator to chill for 20 minutes.

6. Remove from the refrigerator and slice into cookie shape discs, removing the cling film as you do this.

7. Place onto the prepared baking tray and bake for 12–15 minutes until golden brown and still a little chewy. Remove to cool completely and take the ice cream out of the freezer at the same time.

8. To serve scoop the softened ice cream from the tub and place between two cooled cookies.

Grilled pineapple lollies

SERVES: 4-6 | PREP TIME: 30 MINUTES | COOKING TIME: 10 MINUTES

INGREDIENTS

1 pineapple

100 g / 3 ½ oz / ½ cup demerara sugar

2 limes, juiced

METHOD

1. Cut the top and bottom off the pineapple before slicing into wedges vertically.

2. Remove the woody core of the pineapple and cut into lolly shapes and place into a zip lock bag. Add the sugar and lime juices ensuring the fruit is covered evenly.

3. Place into the freezer for around 30 minutes to chill but not freeze completely.

4. Once ready to serve, insert a lolly stick into the base of the pineapple and place onto the hot barbecue or griddle pan and cook until slightly scorched before turning.

Grilled bananas with nuts

SERVES: 2 | PREP TIME: 10 MINUTES | COOKING TIME: 10 MINUTES

INGREDIENTS

2 bananas, peeled and sliced lengthways

1 tsp cinnamon

25 g / 1 oz / ¼ cup walnuts, chopped

2 tbsp maple syrup

100 ml / 3 ⅓ fl. oz / ½ cup double
(heavy) cream, whipped

METHOD

1. Heat the barbecue or griddle to a medium
high heat.

2. Sprinkle the cut side of the bananas with
the cinnamon.

3. Place onto the grill and cook for 8–10 minutes
until charred and warm.

4. Serve with the nuts and syrup drizzled over
the top and cream on the side.

Rum soaked grilled pineapple

SERVES: 4 | PREP TIME: 20 MINUTES | COOKING TIME: 15 MINUTES

INGREDIENTS

1 pineapple

2 tbsp dark brown sugar

75 ml / 2 ½ fl. oz / ⅓ cup dark rum

1 tbsp butter

sprigs of mint to garnish

METHOD

1. Preheat the barbecue to a medium heat.

2. Cut the top and bottom from the pineapple before cutting into wedges. Remove the woody core and place into a flat dish.

3. Melt the sugar, rum and butter together in a saucepan. Once the sugar has melted pour the mixture over the pineapple and mix to coat.

4. Place the pineapple onto the hot grill and cook for 4–6 minutes on each side until charred marks appear. Serve with mint sprigs as garnish

Chocolate brownies

SERVES: 8-10 | PREP TIME: 15 MINUTES | COOKING TIME: 20 MINUTES

INGREDIENTS

100 g / 3 ½ oz dark chocolate

100 g / 3 ½ oz / ½ cup unsalted butter

200 g / 7 oz / ¾ cup caster (superfine) sugar

2 free range eggs, lightly whisked

1 tsp vanilla extract

100 g / 3 ½ oz / 1 cup ground almonds

50 g / 1 ¾ oz / ½ cup cocoa powder

2 tsp baking powder

METHOD

1. Preheat the oven to 180°C (160°C fan) / 350F / gas 4 and grease and line a 20 cm (8 in) square tin.

2. Break the chocolate into pieces and melt gently with the butter in a heat proof bowl over simmering water taking care that the water does not touch the bowl. Remove from the heat and allow to cool.

3. Whisk together the sugar, eggs and vanilla extract until pale and doubled in size. Fold the cooled chocolate mixture into the eggs taking care not to knock out the air.

4. Fold in the ground almonds, cocoa powder, baking powder and salt and mix until all the ingredients are combined.

5. Spread the mixture evenly in the tin and bake in the oven for 15–20 minutes. Leave to cool and cut into 16 even squares.

Blueberry cheesecake

SERVES: 8 | PREP TIME: 45 MINUTES | FREEZING TIME: 4 HOURS

INGREDIENTS

250 g / 9 oz / 1 ½ cups medjool dates, stoned

225 g / 8 oz / 1 ¾ cups walnuts, chopped

250 g / 9 oz / 1 ⅔ cups raw cashew nuts, soaked overnight

400 ml / 14 fl. oz / 2 cup canned coconut milk, chilled unopened

1 ½ lemons, juiced and zest finely grated

75 g / 2 ½ oz ¼ cup runny honey

150 g / 5 oz / 1 cup blueberries

METHOD

1. Soak the dates in warm water for 10 minutes, then drain and transfer to a food processor. Add the chopped walnuts and pulse until it forms a dough. Line a 20 cm (8 in) round spring-form cake tin with cling film, then press the mixture into the base.

2. Drain the cashews and put them in the food processor.

3. Open the can of coconut milk upside down and discard the thin watery layer. Scoop the thick creamy layer into the food processor and add the lemon juice, zest, honey and half the blueberries.

4. Blend until very smooth, pausing to scrape down the sides occasionally. Scrape into the tin and level the top, then cover with cling film. Freeze the cheesecake for at least 4 hours.

5. Remove from the freezer 20 minutes before serving.

6. Unmould the cheesecake and garnish with the rest of the blueberries and some edible flowers.

Lemon meringue tarts

SERVES: 4 | PREP TIME: 45 MINUTES | COOKING TIME: 15 MINUTES

INGREDIENTS

150 g / 5 ¼ oz / 2/3 cup unsalted butter

125 g / 4 ¼ oz / ½ cup caster (superfine) sugar

5 eggs, separated

150 g / 5 ¼ oz / 1 cup plain (all purpose) flour

100 g / 3 ½ oz honey

1 lemon, juice and zest

½ tsp cream of tartar

METHOD

1. Preheat the oven to 200°C (180°C fan) / 400F / gas 6. Lightly grease 4 tart cases.

2. In a bowl cream half of the butter and half of the sugar together until pale and mixed. Gradually mix in two of the egg yolks before adding the flour. Turn out and knead until a smooth dough forms, roll in cling film and place into the refrigerator to rest for 20 minutes.

3. Roll out to 2mm thickness and place into the prepared tart cases, pushing into the corners and trimming off excess. Prick the bases with a fork and line with greaseproof paper weighed down with baking beans. Bake for 12–15 minutes until crisp and golden removing the paper after 10 minutes.

4. For the curd whisk the remaining egg yolks and honey in a saucepan adding the lemon zest. Lower the heat and whisk until thickened and pale yellow. Add the lemon juice and remaining butter, a little at a time, whisking until just starting to bubble. Pass through a sieve and set aside to cool and set.

5. For the meringue, whisk the egg whites and tartar in a stand mixer on high until soft peaks form. Turn down the whisk and gradually add the remaining sugar until thick and glossy.

6. Assemble the cake by spreading the cooled curd over the bases and topping with the meringue. Place under a grill for 5 minutes or until the meringue has started to brown in places.

Pure juice ice lollies

MAKES: 2 OF EACH FLAVOUR | PREP TIME: 15 MINUTES

FREEZING TIME: 4 HOURS

INGREDIENTS

RED LOLLIES:

2 beetroot, quartered

2 red apples, quartered

150 g / 5 ½ oz / 1 cup raspberries

YELLOW LOLLIES:

150 g / 5 ½ oz / 1 cup butternut squash, cubed

1 yellow pepper, quartered

2 mangoes, stoned and cut into chunks

METHOD

1. For each type of lolly, process the ingredients through an electronic juicer, according to the manufacturer's instructions.

2. Divide each type of juice between two holes of a six-hole ice lolly maker.

3. Freeze for 4 hours or until solid before unmoulding and serving.

Fruit salad

SERVES: 4 | PREP TIME: 20 MINUTES | COOKING TIME: 5 MINUTES

INGREDIENTS

150 g / 5 oz / 1 cup strawberries, halved

125 g / 4 ½ oz / 1 cup blackberries

125 g / 4 ½ oz / 1 cup raspberries

100 g / 3 ½ oz / 1 cup blackcurrants

55 g / 2 oz / ½ cup gooseberries

55 g / 2 oz / ½ cup blueberries

55 g / 2 oz / ½ cup redcurrants

2 tbsp caster (superfine) sugar

a small bunch of mint leaves, picked

METHOD

1. Combine all the fruit in a large mixing bowl.

2. Spoon over the sugar and toss lightly to coat; leave to sit for 15 minutes, then divide between bowls.

3. Garnish with the mint leaves before serving. It is delicious served with yogurt and honey.

Cherry sorbet

SERVES: 4 | PREP TIME: 15 MINUTES | FREEZING TIME: 4 HOURS

INGREDIENTS

240 g / 14 oz / 2 ⅔ cups cherries, stoned,
plus 4 whole with stalks

1 tbsp stevia sweetener

1 egg white, lightly beaten

METHOD

1. Put the cherries in the freezer for 3 hours.

2. Transfer the frozen cherries to a food
processor. Add the stevia and then add 50 ml
/ 1 ½ fl oz of water and blend until smooth.
Add the egg white and blend again, then
scrape the mixture into a plastic tub and
freeze for 1 hour.

3. Scoop the sorbet into four glasses and
garnish each one with a whole cherry.

Chocolate marshmallow brownies

SERVES: 9 | PREP TIME: 45 MINUTES | COOKING TIME: 35 MINUTES

INGREDIENTS

100 g / 3 ½ oz / 2/3 cup dark chocolate
(min. 70% cocoa solids), chopped

5 g / 3 oz / ¼ cup unsweetened cocoa powder, sifted

225 g / 8 oz / 1 cup coconut oil

450 g / 1 lb / 2 ½ cups light brown sugar

4 large eggs

110 g / 4 oz / 1 cup self-raising flour

FOR THE TOPPING:

110 ml / 4 fl. oz / ½ cup canned coconut milk

150 g / 5 ½ oz / 1 cup dark chocolate
(min. 70% cocoa solids), finely chopped

2 tbsp coconut oil

75 g / 2 ½ oz / 1 ¼ cups mini marshmallows

METHOD

1. Preheat the oven to 160°C (140°C fan) / 325F / gas 3 and oil and line a 20 cm (8 in) square cake tin with greaseproof paper.

2. Melt the chocolate, cocoa and coconut oil together in a saucepan, then leave to cool a little.

3. Whisk the sugar and eggs together with an electric whisk for 3 minutes or until very light and creamy. Pour in the chocolate mixture and sieve over the flour, then fold it all together until smooth.

4. Scrape into the tin and bake for 35 minutes or until the outside is set, but the centre is still quite soft. Leave to cool completely.

5. To make the topping, put the coconut milk in a small saucepan and heat it gently. Meanwhile, put the chocolate and coconut oil in a mixing bowl. When the coconut milk starts to simmer, pour it over the chocolate in the bowl. Leave to stand for 30 seconds, then stir gently to form a ganache.

6. Spread all but 3 tbsp of the ganache over the brownie and top with marshmallows. Drizzle over the rest of the ganache, then refrigerate for 2 hours or until firm.

INDEX